PRAISE FOR T

"Love is based in understanding, and Don Crosby has made it his life aim to help us understand: ourselves and each other. If you want to be more at peace with yourself and others, if you want help in understanding why you and your loved ones often do what you do and feel what you feel, let Don's words take you by the hand and lead you to a new enlightenment."

—Gary Thomas
Author of *Sacred Marriage* and *A Lifelong Love*

"Experiencing *The Why You Do*, I believe, lies the true power and the gift of Don Crosby's courage and willingness to open his heart and soul to tell his story, to share his struggles so we may more clearly understand ours, as a vital reminder for all of us."

—Dr. Irwin M. Rubin, Author of *The ABC's of Effective Feedback* and *Having It Both Ways: The ABC's of Win-Win Relationships*
Founder/CEO Temenos, Inc.

"Thank you, Don, for helping our family. It was a remarkable experience and you were 'dead on!' As parents of special needs children (autism), the process has given us great insights about our complex family dynamics. You provide a voice to those who cannot effectively communicate, and this book should be another home run for those to understand *The Why You Do*."

—Jim Gott, Pitching Coordinator, Los Angeles Angels of Anaheim
—Cathy Gott, Board Member, Autism Speaks Los Angeles Chapter

"A number of PGA Tour players use sports psychologists to help them deal with their rational game, but their assessment is mostly theory, lacking specifics and missing the understanding of actual human behaviors. Implementing his ProScan® survey, Don Crosby has quickly helped me understand my behaviors and those of my students, which has richly contributed to my mental game. *The Why You Do* will help your golf game and definitely other areas of your life."

—Randy Joyner, PGA Professional and Instructor

"Few things damage the culture of a small business like high employee turnover. If you can reduce that, you will grow and build teamwork and profits much faster. Don Crosby did that for Rose Chauffeured Transportation. *The Why You Do* will not only impact your personal life, but is the secret weapon of how you hire and manage your people."

—HA Thompson, Founder/CEO/Author/Speaker
Rose Chauffeured Transportation, Inc.

"Our church staff, leaders, and congregation were deeply encouraged by our ProScan assessments. Recruiting volunteers to work in our ministry opportunities has become a most enjoyable and rewarding experience. Appreciating and celebrating one another's unique and wonderful personalities have impacted my own family. Understanding *The Why You Do* can change your life and empower your organization."

—Lloyd Bustard, Senior Pastor, Recording Artist,
World Worship Church

THE WHY YOU DO

Dear Justin,

Thank you for your endless support and friendship.

Warmest Regards

[illegible]

2/15

THE WHY

UNLOCKING OUR BEHAVIOR

YOU

TO PREVENT MISUNDERSTANDINGS

DO

DON CROSBY

FOREWORD BY DR. DAVID MOLAPO

Two Harbors Press, Minneapolis

Two Harbors Press
322 First Avenue N, 5th floor
Minneapolis, MN 55401
612.455.2293
www.TwoHarborsPress.com

ISBN-13: 978-1-63413-274-9
LCCN: 2014922608

Distributed by Itasca Books

Cover Design by Alan Pranke
Typeset by B. Cook

Printed in the United States of America

CONTENTS

FOREWORD

Here is a rare chance to find a book that offers sound, practical advice on how to find your purpose in this life.

The Why You Do is an invaluable and extraordinary book. It lays out a simple, step-by-step process by which anyone can discover, pursue, and achieve his or her God-given purpose. My precious friend Don Crosby has penned an incredible, life-changing book that is needed for this generation.

The Why You Do is a book filled with encouragement and wisdom. If you are going through a difficult time, questioning your future, or facing a crisis, this book is for you. It will bring out the glow of hope in times of loneliness and rejection.

The message of the book will definitely strike a chord in every heart. In the first few pages alone, I could relate to these nuggets of truth. I have been privileged to be at various crossroads of life and I wish I knew why I did what I did. However, after gleaning practical advice from this book, I am now empowered to know "the why *I* do."

In this hectic day and age, the foundations of our lives are often overwhelmed by the mundane and routine pressures of life, thus forcing people to pursue shortcuts in achieving success and recognition.

One may not have a life as colorful and challenging as Don Crosby's, but just like him, everyone has a dream ready and waiting to be fulfilled. Remember that "waiting time" is not wasted time. In fact, waiting time is learning time, increasing time, and renewal time.

It is, therefore, refreshing to read Don's book and see his take on our life's passion, potential, and purpose.

Remember, too, that a life without a challenge is a life without strength, and a life without strength is a life without substance. *The Why You Do* will bring out the best in any leader, from the pew to the pulpit, from the corporations to the communities.

If you are at a crossroads, have made some bad choices, experienced pain, face a crisis, or question your future, kindly do yourself a favor—read the book at least fourteen times and digest its contents, and you will be launched into your God-ordained destiny.

Remember that I CAN, YOU CAN, TOGETHER WE CAN be assured of *The Why You Do*.

Dr. David Molapo
President, John Maxwell Co., Africa

PREFACE

How many people truly understand who they are and why they do what they do? How many are curious and desire to learn? Does it take courage to venture into the darkness of the unknown—at any age—to discover why?

To understand, in depth, *The Why You Do* requires understanding the fundamentals of life encompassing a variety of environments—including early childhood experiences, educational influences and experiences, interests, skills and, of course, the natural behavior we've received from the genetic lottery.

My strategy of writing through biography is not to draw attention to myself, but, rather, to carefully share a few of my life experiences in the hope that you, the reader, would personally identify your own experiences and understand how behaviors dictate important outcomes.

The story line moves from my impressionable childhood and family relationships, to adulthood—marriage, education, workplace experiences, church, and community life—while conveying the value of behavior and how it plays an all-encompassing role in our successes and failures.

At the end of these stories is an introduction to a behavioral measurement tool and its inventor, and insight into the academics of its development. This is a summary of the science that makes the tool unique and useful for all ages.

For years, my wife, Kathleen, encouraged me to write my story. On one particularly memorable afternoon, while sipping latte with our friend, author Tim Connor, Tim soberly stated, "Don, you have a book inside you!" From that moment on, I gave myself permission to search inside myself for that book, and the result is an accumulation of more than twelve months of four o'clock mornings.

A few years ago, on the unpredictable journey of hosting a radio talk show and moving from guest to guest, I wondered, "Is anyone really listening?" Soon, one of my loyal listeners became a guest, who happily morphed into one of my closest friends. Because of her contributions of time and remarkable talent, this book is a reality. You are an extraordinary friend, Gail Peplinski.

From the early years of broadcasting, audiences have followed radio and TV personalities and their humorous—and sometimes painful—identities. I have learned from them that the behavioral influence of our family, friends, and acquaintances on our own life contributes to our potential for happy memories or painful regrets.

The hilarious and brilliant comedy of *I Love Lucy* (a weekly TV show that lit up the 50s and can now be found in syndication) has entertained generations of people because they could identify with its quirky characters Lucy, Ricky, Fred, and Ethel. With each syndicated episode, Lucy and Ricky continue to welcome us into their lives, and give us permission to laugh at ourselves and our imperfections. There is something special about how we connect with them, as if we're all part of a universal family. It could be that there is a little bit of them in each of us. You will find there is a little bit of each of you in my book, as well. Our stories are similar.

The purpose of this book is to be an inspiration—a snapshot of one man's introspective journey into his heart and soul. By sharing insights from my years of untangling the intricacies of personal behavior, as well as from my fellowship with the developer of the powerful ProScan®[1] tool, which is a behavioral assessment technology, I have invoked my passion for serving others.

This book is intended to be a fluid, heartfelt read, filled with encouragement for the reader to enrich his or her understanding of "the why you do what you do," and help all to accept, develop, and love the one you're with.

Written for days such as these.

Don Crosby

"The two most important days in your life are the day you are born and the day you find out why."
-- Mark Twain

---

1 ProScan®, PDP®, Professional DynaMetric Programs®, are registered trademarks of PDP®, Inc.

LETTER TO THE READER

Don Crosby's book, *The Why You Do* is for every person who has ever wondered, "Why in the world do I do what I do?" and compared themselves with their friends and family in the process.

As someone with a PhD in psychology, 180+ hours of post-doctoral clinical studies, who is a Charter Faculty Instructor of the Myers Briggs Type Indicator, and who has many years of clinical practice, I am naturally skeptical of the do-it-yourself use of personality assessments by untrained persons. I have witnessed well-intentioned lay individuals fail while attempting to employ "Type Psychology" (i.e., the Myers-Briggs Type Indicator, DISC, Four Personality types, etc.) to explain everything from schizo-affective disorder to congenital anomalies.

My first experience witnessing Don at work was in a lunch seminar with about forty business people. I showed up to the meeting as a skeptic, but I quickly observed that Don has an incredible perspicacity and an incredible tool in his ProScan Behavioral Assessment! He has honed his craft and integrated the parameters of the assessment tool in such a way as to soar past others in the field of behavioral psychology. Moreover, he has done so with respect and a non-judgmental demeanor which honors the person he is working with!

I am so glad he has written this book. *The Why You Do* connects the reader to his or her inner self. Don's self-administered reflective analysis helps you gain incredible insight quickly, efficiently, and accurately! His twenty-five years of experience and his genuine concern for people places him into an elite group of behavioral science colleagues—one that gets results! After spending a few minutes with Don, you will be amazed at his laser-sharp focus and the way he will "introduce you to yourself, your partner, or your team members."

Don Crosby's book, *The Why You Do* is not the warm and fuzzy "parlor game fodder" from the 1970s—this is behavioral science brought into the twenty-first century by a passionate practitioner with a real gift for understanding people—and more importantly, helping them to understand themselves. I unreservedly recommend this book and its author to you!

William L. Wiley, PhD, MBA, AIF
Partner and Wealth Advisor
Stratos Wealth Partners-Carolinas, LLC

SECTION ONE
PERSONAL IDENTITY

Every individual's core belief structure consists of their personal identity and history of successes and failures. Chapters 1-6 illustrate a variety of the most common personal and experiential environments.

CHAPTER 1

EVERYONE HAS A STORY

"It is only in adventure that some people succeed in knowing themselves—in finding themselves."
-- Andre Gide

Regardless of where one was born or raised, or the type of family dynamic they inherited, everyone has a story.

Naturally, the story begins when we are very young, but no one knows our deepest feelings—our hurts, our expectations, or our dreams—because we are just kids full of boundless energy, mischief, and careless abandon. Spending precious time thinking about what happened yesterday or what might be in our lunch box tomorrow, is a waste, right?

For me, it was quite different. Ever since childhood, I have been a thinker. By quietly studying the people surrounding my young life I was fascinated. My mind frequently wandered away from my own reality into the dangerously uncharted territory of comparing myself to others. I realized that everyone had their own stories, but they did not seem as concerned about the outcome as I was. They seemed to live in the moment, while I pondered the truth of their realities.

Trying to understand the behavior of others compared to my own behavior started to consume me. By meditating with this mentality, the most rewarding lesson I learned was that understanding my story was less important than my ultimate vocation of being able to help others to understand theirs. My only regret is that it took me so many years and experiences.

How many children really understand their emotional compass? During what stage of life does adulthood actually express emotional intelligence? It occurred to me that just because one's biological clock indicates "adulthood," it does not render him or her an expert at understanding people or life.

My story began early, as I mentioned above. At what stage of life did your story begin? When was your moment of deepest revelation?

My father, J. E. Crosby, bought our 160-acre mint farm in the little Michigan town of St. Johns (which is located about eighteen miles north of Lansing), when I was just two years old.

The town was an attractive place to raise a family. The storybook setting of a Midwestern "Mayberry" offered the classic environment where everyone knew your parents and grandparents so you did not have much measure for error. You had better be on your best behavior, or you could become common news.

Our simple lifestyle played out distinctly opposite of that which seemed to be ingrained in my DNA. I was an ambitious, sometimes-hopeless dreamer. What seemed like a life sentence in rural Michigan was growing up with the responsibility of having to do chores and feed the animals. I never thought for a minute that I would ever miss or reminisce about my chores. During the summer, when other kids were off having fun, my brother and I were on the farm with something to do all the time. As any farmer knows, when working the ground, the work is never done. You go from field to field, from spring to harvest and, in the fall, you plow it up to begin again. The bitterly cold winters brought drifting snow that required endless shoveling, and the sticky, hot summers brought a new set of challenges. Whatever the season, the animals still needed to be fed twice a day, while the fields beckoned for attention until the last drops of energy drained from our tired bodies.

The work was hard, but life was simple. All I wanted to do was play baseball or softball. After all, I was sure I was going to be a professional baseball player, and all I needed to do was practice. I did not see the importance of farm work—or even school work—because grades and education were the least important items on my list of priorities. All I needed was an excellent batting average and the ability to horizontally stretch out in a full-speed, unobstructed sprint to dive for the catch of a hard-hit fly ball.

Every child needs an exceptional role model and my only non-family hero was Detroit Tiger number six, right fielder Al Kaline. The excitement of watching the Tigers fueled my ambition to be a ballplayer. I loved the Tigers and even enjoyed following the Yankees and the White Sox. However, I did not feel the same hero reverence with the other players that I felt for Kaline. Watching him express his athletic ability in fielding, hitting, and pure teamwork was inspiring—but there was another attraction. He possessed a pleasantly understated charm—a recognizable substance of character as a gentlemen and true champion—both on and off the field. One of the aspects of "hero worship" is based upon the behavior of the "hero".

> How is behavior developed? It is apparent to anyone who has observed small children that very early in life, infants exhibit certain behavioral traits that appear to be inherited. During an individual's early years, future values imprinted through behavioral modeling. Permanent values are established based upon such environmental factors as family, friends, religion, education, and media. Social and monetary attitudes, coping behaviors, gender roles and prejudices all contribute to the developing value system.
>
> During pre-teen years, "hero worship" is a very important value influence. The socialization process locks in

> permanent values and creates the specific method used by each individual to achieve life's goals.
>
> According to the work of Dr. Morris Massey, only a significant emotional event can modify these perceptions. (Ref. People Puzzle, Morris Massey Associates)[2]

During the springs and summers of my youth, I stayed with my grandparents in town as often as possible so I could ride my bike everywhere in search of ballgames to plug into. When not in a ballgame, I thrived on the company of Grandpa Bruno and Grandma Arge. We became inseparable friends, and, in them, I found another set of parents. A few years later, Bruno suffered a stroke, and my time with my grandparents moved from my personal time of playing baseball to care giving.

Several days into the summer vacation after fifth grade, my dreams of riding into town to find a ballgame were suddenly extinguished by a gasoline fire. The process of what happened is a longer story than the outcome—a one-quart coffee can full of gasoline spilled onto my right pants leg while I was helping my younger brother start a camp fire. The flames shot up underneath my blue jeans, scorching my skin with third-degree burns.

I remember lying in my hospital bed near an open window, somewhere in between the accident and my recovery, listening to other kids outside chattering with excitement about where they were going and how they would spend their summer vacations. Oh, it was so hard to think of fun, amidst the physical pain and uncertainty of my healing process.

While they were talking of games, I was wondering if the skin grafting from my left thigh would actually take care of itself, or if I would suffer below-the-knee amputation. The emotional and physical trauma I experienced that summer was nearly unbearable for a kid who was so passionate about playing ball. My new challenge was not run-

---

2 PDP Research Reference Manual, Copyright 1984, rev. 2011, Page 1

ning to catch the ball; but learning how to walk again and regain my strength. I knew I could overcome this setback because, by the grace of God, my leg had been spared. I just had to learn how to use it again.

I did not feel better until the next summer, almost a year to the day. One afternoon, while playing in the front yard, I decided to climb up a thick barn rope, which had been tied securely for years to a hickory tree. Just as I was about to reach the top, the old, weather-worn rope snapped and I plummeted to the ground, landing on my elbow and sustaining a severe fracture. This playful misfortune landed me in the hospital again, for thirty days of traction, and the rest of the hot summer was spent with my elbow in a cast. In those days, physical therapy was an unknown art, and we just coped with difficult situations as they came along.

Due to my two consecutive summers of injury and hospitalization, I spent those critical years of growing and developing important strength and muscle mass simply lying in bed trying to heal from not only the pain and misfortune, but also from the knowledge that—even after I was healed—I could only dream of playing baseball.

Intertwined with my physical pain and weakened ambition was the fear of my parents separating and possibly becoming divorced. A few years earlier, they had taken me for a ride and broken the news that they were having problems in their marriage. They were considering a separation, which eventually led to my mother going to San Francisco to visit her sister. I was so young that I do not recall how long she was gone, only that she did return. My fears of their possible divorce tormented me as I tried to focus on healing my body and I could not stop worrying about my family security.

When my father tried to explain what was happening, I was too young to understand the complete effect their troubles would have on me later. The only thing I was sure of was how I was feeling. I experienced deep sadness as I absorbed the painful words being exchanged by my parents during that time. Mom and Dad eventually accrued twenty-eight years together before finally divorcing. Though I worried about it as a pre-teen, their break-up was not during my childhood, but when I was twenty-four years old and living in Alaska. My youngest brother, however, Jim was only ten, and I regret that I was not there to comfort him.

During my formative years of social maturing and educational development, I graduated from a one-room schoolhouse in the country, to a public school in town. I shared all of my early school years with nineteen other kids—including my younger brother, Mark, and little sister, Linette—but I was alone in my class.

When I went from sharing my class with no one in that one-room schoolhouse, to taking the bus into town to join forty other children in my homeroom, I met challenges I had never expected. This was an era when neither parents nor school officials were sophisticated enough to prepare children to cope with abnormal social situations—not to mention the emotional setback of two consecutive summer vacations in the hospital.

I have learned, over time, that we can choose to spend our time reminiscing about what we do or do not have, or we can accept our circumstances and believe in ourselves so that we can move forward with faithful determination and a strong work ethic. Determination and good work ethics were characteristic of both sides of my family, so, from this perspective, I was surely blessed with good genes.

In my professional life, I have counseled and heard a wide array of amazing and heart-wrenching stories, which have taken people from rags to riches, and back to rags. There have been folks with sad medical issues and financial crossroads, problems with children, and homelessness. If you can imagine it, I have probably heard a story about it.

A common denominator in my conversations with all of these people has been hearing about bad decisions, bad things that were happening to good people, or the consequences of bad decisions that were intended for good, but had disastrous results. To be more specific, our own will and decisions create life-altering outcomes. Thus, the "wish-I-would-haves" and "wish-I-could-haves" evolve with regret, sadness, low self-esteem, depression, and sometimes-fatal outcomes.

We are all prisoners of our own behaviors, whether brilliant or lackluster, and we all have a story resonating from our childhood, health, family, career, finances, education, and life experiences.

Your story is important, as many families are unaware of the accomplishments and dynamics of their own loved ones. Typically, the perspective of a person is lacking the identity of who they are as a person, and understanding "the why they do" what they do.

Thankfully, I have rich childhood memories of my parents, grandparents, aunts, and uncles in the prime of their lives, which have given me a treasure chest of information to draw on, and which have enhanced my appreciation for the circumstances in my life. They have truly helped me to embrace my early story.

Chapter Nugget

If you missed out on strong parenting during your childhood, the opportunity is yours to break the dysfunctional cycle and become an exceptional role model. Hold and teach your children like the precious and unique little people they are. If you do this well, they will never know the misfortunes you suffered.

"How old would you be if you didn't
know how old you were?"
-- Satchel Paige

CHAPTER 2

IN THE EARLY YEARS OF LIFE

"In every dispute between parent and child, both cannot be right, but they may be, and usually are, both wrong. It is this situation, which gives family life its peculiar hysterical charm."
-- Isaac Rosenfeld

When you were a small child, how many times did someone tell you to change your behavior? *Be quiet! Don't do that! Straighten up!* Maybe it was the result of something you said, or something you did—a mere behavioral reaction to things going on around you. As you grew older, it seemed to happen more often, and finally you began to wonder "Is it me? What is wrong with me? I really did not mean it that way! Why am I such a mess? Is there any use to keep trying?"

For too many years, kids have suffered repercussions from feeling as if they were a mistake. Upon entering adulthood, they have found themselves still holding onto these negative feelings.

As a young boy, my dad was the victim of harsh, verbal criticism from his sick grandfather. Along with his illness, dad's grandfather had a very insensitive disposition, and was constantly admonishing my dad to be silent. Because my grandparents had moved in to care for my great-grandfather, dad was now suffering along with his grandfather. Later on in his life, Dad shared the stories of some of those experiences with me.

The oldest of three boys, Dad was scolded so much by his grandfather that he was unable to just "be a kid" around the house. Consequently, he had conformed to being a quiet man who struggled within himself, uncomfortable to integrate with others. As I grew up and began to learn about Dad's youthful experiences, I could not understand his quiet demeanor. What bothered me even more was that he did not talk with me about the usual "father/son stuff", like hunting and fishing. Even so, Dad was a smart, mild-mannered man who was very hard on himself. Thinking about him and his reticence is, for me, another example of how we are all prisoners of our own minds.

I recall that, one Michigan morning, we were hit with a hard frost that ruined our entire soybean crop. The day before had been nothing short of bucolic, filled with the promise of a record year ahead. Who knew that the next day would bring total devastation—that our green fields would suddenly fade to brown? My poor father's mood soon resembled the color of our failed crop. It was sad to see him in that state of decline.

Later that afternoon, coming home from school, I spotted our family's '57 Chevy parked along the windbreak of willow trees in one of our ruined fields. The door on the driver's side was open wide. I saw what appeared to be the glowing overhead dome light, and I became full of fear. I had to get to the car as fast as I could. Not taking the time to hop on the tractor, I raced through the field on foot, filled with dread. Would I find that he had taken his own life?

My heart was pounding and, as I ran, my feet seemed unable to keep pace with my emotions. Dad was the epitome of a good man. He was the real thing—an exceptional farmer, a hard worker who calculated his strategy and worked within a budget. Had he pushed himself too far? How was I going to find him when I reached the car?

When I finally got to him, I found him lying face down in the front seat, head on the passenger side, one leg on the driver's seat and the other leg dangling over the steering wheel. On the floor were five empty beer cans, with only one full can remaining of the six-pack. That sight only exacerbated my fears.

I cried out, because at that point, I did not know what was going on. I will never forget the expression on his face when he looked up. His tone was a mixture of embarrassment and anger, and then he proceeded to loudly accuse me of violating his privacy. He said that he needed his space and wanted to be alone. Walking back to the house, heartsick yet relieved that my greatest fears had not materialized, I worried that there might be a next time.

Year after year, Mother and I watched as something would eventually prevent my Dad from success. He tried again, but something always went wrong. He would retreat into his quiet shell and beat himself up. This process was hard to watch for a family that was so in love with their Dad.

Mother was always the encourager—the one who told me to reach for my dreams and that there were no limitations for the dreamer. They were both good, solid parents, but their behaviors were diametrically opposed—as different as day and night.

It is regrettable that my great-grandfather had no appreciation for how his behavior was affecting my dad's life. If only he could have explained to Dad in a nurturing way how he was feeling. If so, how would Dad's behavior have been different? What kind of an effect would it have had on Dad's self-esteem, his success, and our family?

Dad thought that, surely, something was wrong with him because of the problems associated with our lifestyle and the fact that he just could not get a break. Our farm was beautiful, though, from a child's perspective—little seemed to be missing in our lives, other than for Dad to work one (instead of two) jobs, and the fact that he never had a new pickup truck.

Unfortunately, during my teen years where I really needed my father I did not really know him. In fact, I was sure he did not like me, and the feeling of distance between us seemed so great that I wanted to believe that he must have at least loved me. I simply wanted to know why he did not *like* me.

My early recollections of my father tell me that he always chose to do other things rather than spend time with his young son. His broken promises, which resulted in missing the first days of hunting season, neglecting sporting events and so much more, were among my disappointments. It seemed as if he was intentionally avoiding being involved in my childhood. (For example, it was my mother who surprised me one Friday night by introducing me to my first high school football game.)

I felt emotionally detached from him and we did not really have a relationship until I was about thirty-seven years of age. Why, in such a nice home and family as ours when I was young, would there have been such misunderstanding? It is often said that "we are not all perfect."

Even though we had a fairly non-existent relationship, my father and I were able to start over when he completed his unplanned ProScan behavioral assessment. The process of comparing our behaviors broke the ice and, for the first time, I really understood my father. And, for the first time, he really understood me. My only response was to request his forgiveness for my past behaviors. From that moment, we began to develop a father-and-son relationship.

Have you ever felt flawed? Have you ever questioned your personal identity? Have you ever wondered why you do what you do? Have you ever asked yourself these questions? We all have a story. I now have a deep appreciation for the series of events that brought forth my reconciliation with my father, and how it changed the last fifteen years of our lives together.

My dad was bullied as a child in his own home, and no one realized the effect it would have on him. For many families, this behavior is common and the failure of families to communicate with each other has become epidemic. Feeling flawed can be a good example of having been bullied. Depending on how socially impaired a person may become from this experience, combined with the source and timing of the torment, some people may never recover.

I remember the torment of a close friend who was bullied in the eighth grade. What compounded his situation was the way in which he allowed himself to have a poor self-image *prior to* the antagonizing torture from the other kids. When the bullying started, it did not take much to push him over the edge into severe depression. How many other situations are similar to his? How many children and adults do we lose each year because of poor self-esteem?

Oddly, when I was growing up, our home had other issues, and at one time I was the contributor. My brother, Mark, and I were very different. His energy was lower than mine. I needed someone to play with, and he was happy to sit alone and read. We simply had different interests. My problem was that I truly believed he would not play with me because I was just his brother, and so I took it as a personal rejection. I just could not come to grips with the fact that, yes, he was my brother, but we had different interests. Remember, we were very young, reacting to how our little minds were processing, but being youthful did not dismiss the pain and frustration.

Because we lived out in the country and our farm was miles from any other children, the need for my brother to join me in a game of catch to sharpen my baseball skills was obvious. To my young mind, there was only one possible explanation: Why would he not oblige me, unless he really did not like me? Looking back, I can see that our unique differences did not mean one of us was superior, it only meant that our lack of interaction should have been predictable, given our natural behaviors.

Our needs and motivators were so distant, however, that they formed a wedge in our relationship and my brother and I did not even know why we failed to get along as siblings. How could we have brotherly love and not get along? At times, he made me so mad that we would fight like two bear cubs. One afternoon, within minutes of finishing a brawl, I was pedaling my bike up the back sidewalk thinking everything was fine. Suddenly, my brother swung open the door at precisely the moment of my arrival. I smashed through the door, shattering glass, bashing my head, and wondering what had happened. Although dazed with thoughts of his action being retaliation, I knew it was an accident. Reflecting on that playful escapade, I know that my brother would never have been vindictive because his heart is too kind.

All too frequently, there is news about brothers hurting or killing one or the other over meaningless differences. My brother and I have a lot to be thankful for, having never come to that deadly extreme. I did not realize how badly I had hurt him—though not physically—until my mid-adult years. Since then, I have tried numerous times—and in different ways—to tell him how deeply I regret the actions of my youth.

If only I could have understood "why" we were so naturally different when I was younger, I would have forgotten about my own feelings and done some of the things that he liked to do.

We did not know that our childhood arguments were normal, based upon the genetic lottery of the behaviors we received at birth. We both simply acted out our feelings because of our natural design. Unfortunately, because of our differences, we deduced that each of us was intentionally trying to do the other wrong.

The well-known saying, "sticks and stones will break my bones, but words will never hurt me", is a myth. Offensive words cut deep and all behaviors are subjected to offense. Keep in mind that puppy love is real to the puppy.

Our lives in general begin with the slap of the doctor's hand on our backside. During childhood, our life accelerates, and the teen years become a blur. Soon we awaken as adults, engulfed in responsibilities within the family, the workplace, and the community. We discover that, in order to get along with others, change is required. Wow! We need to change. Imagine what happens when the very behavior modifications we were tired of hearing about are now exactly what we need to be perfect.

Has anyone ever told you that you need to change? Maybe your parents or grandparents, teachers, scout leaders, staff sergeants, bosses, or ex-spouses tried to change you. If so, you probably have an unpleasant video playing repeatedly in your head. If someone told you that you needed to change, chances are you would resist. In fact, you may even have been offended, and a long-term estrangement to your friendship may have resulted. Whatever the scenario, when we hear that we need to change, we are really hearing that we need to work to eliminate our flaws.

Change represents a long-term unnatural commitment, as opposed to a simple adjustment, which merely represents a short-term, acceptable commitment. When we hear the word "adjustment," it resonates to a lesser degree of criticism and, therefore, we are often more willing to adjust than to change. (Which one do you prefer?)

Our past failures to change have no bearing on who we are, how much we have, or the combined pain and happiness we have experienced. Moving forward, our social success is dependent upon our ability—both consciously and subconsciously—to permit ourselves to adjust our natural behaviors periodically to a variety of real-life experiences.

Today, more than ever, we need to understand who we are to be able to stabilize how we think, act, react and treat others, as well as how we treat ourselves. Maybe we even need to treat ourselves with greater dignity.

Relax and seek understanding. Our behavioral reactions have the ability to make or break our relationships so quickly that we may not know what happened, and the subsequent repercussions could be endless.

The personal advantage of learning about "the why we do what we do," without fear and condemnation of being a flawed human being, is priceless. Who says we need to change? Perhaps we just need to understand ourselves and make adjustments based on our situations, our responsibilities, and those with whom we are dealing.

Chapter Nugget

One sure way of reinforcing a healthy family is by learning how to clearly recognize behavioral differences in each of its members. Exhibit an appreciation for each person by loving them for their uniqueness. Use a thoughtful approach to let them know they are special. Realize that with each difference come myriad special abilities. If this is missing in your home, your children may never know how exceptional they are, and may seek acceptance in the wrong places.

"I cannot teach anybody anything;
I can only make them think."
-- Socrates

CHAPTER 3

DO I REALLY KNOW MY FAMILY?

"A hero is one who does what he can."
-- Romain Rolland

My grandfather, Bruno Mazzolini, was, quite simply, a thoughtful man. One of his true gifts in life was his ability to "think ahead" about the people he would be meeting on any given day. He was permanently prepared with an arsenal of items he took with him wherever he went. He always remembered the little things that made such a difference—a simple pack of Wrigley's Juicy Fruit or Spearmint gum, a Hershey bar, or the soft drinks he routinely stowed in the back of his faded green 1946 Ford pickup truck. Grandpa Bruno was not only a "people magnet"—even animals could not forget him. (One of his rituals was a stop at the butcher shop for bones to give the pets he would meet along the way.) He, himself, was the only advertising "Bruno's Wonder Bar" ever needed—he was a brand unto himself, and brought in all of the patrons that his bar needed.

He gave without an ulterior motive. His generosity was the fabric of who he was. His success was rooted in his charitable acts, and—somehow—he would always devise another business transaction to make a little more money to replace what he gave away. Grandma Arge worked very hard alongside him with seldom a weekend off. She attributed their lack of finances to his lifestyle. Although he loved the 1946 Ford truck he drove around to give out his treats, by 1953, Bruno had purchased twenty-seven new Buicks from his friend, Smithie, who owned the local Buick dealership. Smithie's was, conveniently, within walking distance of Bruno's Wonder Bar.

When the local newspaper featured Bruno receiving the keys to his 1953 Golden Anniversary Sedan, his comment included Buick's own advertising slogan: "Naturally it is the greatest Buick in fifty years, because 'when better automobiles are built, Buick will build them.'"

Bruno bought cars as if they were his favorite cigars. I always wondered if it could have been the convenience of the car dealership—and the influence of alcohol—that prompted all these purchases. On one particular occasion, he bought a new 1950 two-tone Buick sedan, got drunk, and totaled the car before Grandma Arge ever knew they were the proud new owners of the car. He got a ride home that night and, when he woke up the next morning, he called Smithie to replace the wrecked car with an identical one. (For years, only a few of Grandpa's closest friends knew that he had owned two cars in less than twenty-four hours.)

Grandma Arge earned her reputation as a culinary master in our small town of St. Johns, Michigan. Although she was not formally trained, she had a gift for producing a gastronomical feast from the simplest of ingredients. Both she and Grandpa Bruno were chefs in their own rite—not unlike the fiercest competitors on the Food Network today. Of Italian heritage, they were also unquestionably Roman Catholic, which flavored our lives in more ways than their cooking ever could.

As a kindergartener, I could not understand why Church "royalty"—i.e., visiting priests, cardinals, and bishops from daily Mass—would eventually make their way to Grandma Arge's kitchen for lunch or dinner. I do not recall them ever sitting in our formal dining room;

rather, they congregated in our small kitchen like family from the "old country." I, a "serious little Catholic" who loved God and had the deepest respect for the Church and its Holy Sacraments, found it so cool that I could sit at the table with these elite church leaders. It was like hosting a rock star. I am not sure whether it was Grandma Arge's flavorful dishes, or Grandpa Bruno's bartending skills—or both—that attracted them.

Frequently, Grandma would serve mounds of spaghetti paired with roast chicken, large bowls of garden salad, and freshly baked Italian bread. Each meal was a feast, with fascinating stories and loving fellowship. We each had a role in the hospitality department. Often, my job was to run down to the basement to fetch more wine, because Grandpa would keep their glasses filled with Chianti. As the conversation became happier, Grandma would get mad at Grandpa for serving too much *vino*. (In fact, on several occasions, as soon as our guests left, Grandpa received a scolding, with Grandma telling him that he was "going to Hell for getting these holy men drunk!") These are wonderful memories and I sometimes ponder what stories of my amazing Grandma Arge and Grandpa Bruno might have filtered back to Italy.

In December of 1959, during my first-grade year in Catholic school, our class was selling Christmas cards as a fundraiser. The first-place prize was a four-inch ceramic statue of Jesus holding a lamb in his arms.

Something happened to me when I saw that statue—I identified myself as the lamb and, in my heart, I knew that I needed to "win" Jesus. That evening at the dinner table, I could hardly eat as I described to my parents how I was going to do this. From that point on, I shared my feelings with anyone who would listen. If my memory is correct, my mother, Mary, drove me to a few neighborhoods so I could tell my story door to door. What I eventually learned was that making sales was much easier if I simply made random calls on my friends and the patrons of Bruno's Wonder Bar since I spent so much time there.

Life in the bar was quite satisfying for a seven-year-old boy. The camaraderie was comparable to having a large group of happy uncles playing shuffleboard every day and teaching the art of shooting pool. Moreover, the burgers that came off the grill were amazing. Bruno definitely knew how to make burgers, to this day, just thinking about them makes me forget everything I ever learned about healthy eating.

Regardless of the fun I had in Bruno's bar, I simply had to have that statue of Jesus. I have no idea how good I was at selling Christmas cards—all I knew was that I had fallen in love and was sure I must have sold enough cards to win a life-size replica of Jesus. What a contrast—from playing games in Bruno's Wonder Bar to needing to win a statue of Jesus—so I could have God. Think about it—I thought I had to *win* Jesus. I did not know about having a personal relationship with Him without having to go through the exercise of selling Christmas cards. (After all, if "having God," meant winning a Christmas card contest, Hallmark would surely own the Church.)

1st Place Prize, author's personal photo

My own young personality and behavior were developing through the love I had for Grandpa Bruno. We were inseparable—I was his miniature shadow and we enjoyed precious times together that few others could understand. Unfortunately, along with Bruno's successful people skills, his time in the bar unwittingly uncovered alcoholism. The sickness that he could not understand interrupted his fun-loving disposition and propensity for telling stories. Eventually, it contributed to a stroke and, after three ensuing years of suffering, death.

The curious circumstances of Grandma Arge's years of financial worry were discovered during the process of Bruno's funeral. The flowers that arrived were only a small token in comparison to the stream of praise for Grandpa Bruno. People began telling my grandmother how Bruno had supplied multiple families with baby food, diapers, and baby beds. He had paid medical bills and helped countless others get through their hardships. He even helped save some families from losing their farms by paying off their mortgages.

Grandpa Bruno gave unselfishly to others, even when his own family was in need, but he was confident that he could always find a way to make enough money to go around. I remember grandma's emotional reaction when she first heard the stories from husbands, wives, and widows. She had mixed emotions—she was angry that her husband had not told her about his benevolent acts, while at the same time, she was proud of him for supporting so many families.

Grandpa Bruno was a man who had no sales training. He had arrived in America in 1909 as a teenage immigrant just after finishing high school. He only had his family and a few relatives—and an uncompromising spirit of optimism and passion. An article was written in the Clinton County *Republication-News* on September 15, 1955, of Grandpa Bruno's and Grandma Arge's trip back to Italy after 46 years. In the article the writer references Grandpa Bruno as "There is much which Horatio Alger success stories in the life of Bruno Mazzolini."[3]

He innocently believed that if he worked hard enough and applied himself, he could fulfill his destiny. And, in those days, that seemed to be enough. I remember him exclaiming to me, "If you ever need

---

3 Clinton County *Republican-News* (St. Johns, MI), September 15, 1955, 1.

money, all you have to do is sell hotdogs. Everybody likes a good hotdog!" Maybe I missed my calling by not opening "Bruno's Hotdog Carts" during my early adulthood.

Bruno on motorcycle, 1911, Ionia, Michigan, photo from the author's family album

The world's economic successes are an accumulation of thousands of stories like Bruno's, each rich with a variety of old-world traditions. Many families had a Bruno, but are sadly unaware of that fact as the stories die with the generations. We need to remember that our greatest inheritance is not our ancestors' property and possessions, but the legacy of who they were.

Their trip to their homeland in Barga, in the county of Florence, fulfilled several purposes—revisiting family and friends, enjoying the food, wine, and culture, and simply vacationing away from their business and social pressures. Nevertheless, these purposes were all secondary, because truly they were looking forward to returning to the opera.

Grandpa loved the opera, and classical music—to him—was as sacred as the Catholic Church.

Two of their five children made names for themselves in the field of classical music. Uncle Joe, at the time thirty-three years of age, had just completed three and a half years of advanced study in Rome, and would be making his debut as a tenor at the Rome Opera on October 2, 1955, with his proud parents sitting in the audience. Aunt Brunetta, thirty years old and a soprano, was already on tour in Europe with an opera concert group, and would be meeting up with Grandpa, Grandma, and Uncle Joe.

(Early one morning, while writing this very chapter, I was stunned to hear Uncle Joe's voice on the Turner Classic Movie channel. Glancing up from my computer screen, I saw Uncle Joe singing in the opening scenes of *Escape Me Never*, the 1947 film with Errol Flynn and Ida Lupino. Uncle Joe had sung in many movies, but made Italy his choice over Hollywood.)

While on their trip in Italy Grandpa Bruno's prized memento was the investment of a gold watch and chain. Aunt Brunetta inherited the watch and thoughtfully knew how important Grandpa Bruno was to me, so she had his watch cleaned and refurbished, with the intention of presenting it to me. Unfortunately, her home in Portland, Oregon, was burglarized and the watch was among the many items taken. I recall her horror as she recounted the story of the home intrusion. Although I was shaken by her loss, my fond memories of Bruno carrying his watch—and Brunetta's intended generosity—were more of a blessing to me than the watch itself.

Bruno's eccentric lifestyle succeeded with ease in the early and mid-1900s. However, realizing that the world's standards have fundamentally changed, how would Bruno do business today? Bruno was an interesting guy who offered a unique perspective on life—and, just like Bruno, we all have our own stories, brimming with life's experiences and lessons.

We make choices that ultimately cause the success or failure of our lives. Grandpa Bruno was a very successful man, but, sadly, his alcoholism destroyed his role as a husband and father, while shaving years off his life.

Chapter Nugget

Instead of being impressed with the accomplishments of people you don't know, discover the special accomplishments of your family members. Your relatives may or may not have held impressive positions or obtained great fame, but everyone's story is interesting and important to the rest of the family. Question your relatives and document their experiences for future generations. Remember, people with the quietest demeanor may be reluctant to reveal their stories so be persistent.

"Now that it is all over, what did you really do yesterday that's worth mentioning?"
-- Coleman Cox

CHAPTER 4

WHAT IF THERE WERE NO DREAMERS?

My Father's Grandfather
The back forties are separated by
Great Grandfather's wooden bridge.
Like Great Grandpa, weather-beaten by years,
needs more attention now.
The boards are aged—even my pony cannot cross.
As for Great Grandpa, he left us years ago, but not
before teaching us a bond for family love.
Greatness his children knew, a specialty
the grandchildren would learn.
And now, no one can ever replace the boards of
Great Grandfather's wooden bridge.

Consider how life in the United States would be if the early settlers had been without ambition. What if higher ideals were nonexistent, and mediocrity was the accepted, normal lifestyle? Where would this country be without innovation, ingenuity, and excellence? As we celebrate the accomplishments of our ancestors, we realize the efforts which were required under their extreme circumstances, to not only survive, but also create, innovate, and industrialize our nation. We marvel at their determination to succeed, and we greatly admire the passion and motivation that made our country great.

If you could have just one wish—the ability to understand the behavior of your ancestors—what similarities do you think you would share with them? Would this inspire you to have a passion to succeed? How many times have you looked yourself in the mirror and wondered how your grandmother or grandfather might have gotten through the particular challenges you are now facing? What types of problems might the generations before us have encountered?

My father's grandfather and namesake, J. E. Crosby, Sr. lost everything during the greatest cataclysm that ever struck the great state of Ohio. From March 23 to March 27, 1913, the death and destruction caused by the Flood of 1913 exceeded all other weather events in Ohio history, earning it the title "Ohio's Greatest Weather Disaster." Rainfall over the state totaled six to eleven inches with no region spared. The death toll was four hundred sixty-seven, and according to records kept by the Ohio Historical Society, more than forty thousand homes were flooded. "In Dayton, the Great Miami River flooded fourteen square miles of the city as its murky and deadly waters rushed in swift currents ten feet deep through downtown streets. The flood killed one hundred twenty-three people in Dayton that year."[4]

As a result of that flood, Great Grandpa Crosby lost his entire business and plunged into bankruptcy. As an affluent dairy farmer, he had raised cows, run a milking operation, and delivered the fresh, creamy, white goodness to homes and businesses. Today, he would be considered an entrepreneur—but, then, he was just a farmer and milkman, driven by his desire to support and care for his family.

4 "1913 Statewide Flood," *Ohio History Connection*, accessed June 30, 2014, http://ww2.ohiohistory.org/etcetera/exhibits/swio/pages/content/1913_flood.htm.

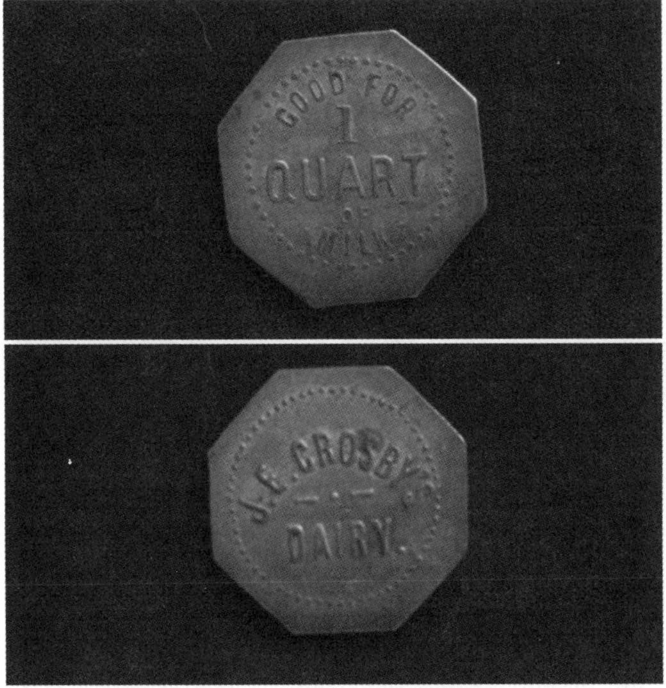

J. E. Crosby's Dairy, free milk token, 1910,
photo taken by the author.

Thereafter, the forty-four-year-old, tired, broken, and discouraged dairy farmer watched as his disease-stricken cows perished. What must have been going through his mind? How was he able to cope with this disaster?

My family never knew why he eventually migrated to St. Johns, Michigan—only that he arrived with only a wagon, a few pieces of furniture, and a small amount of livestock to re-establish a life for his family. Sometime later, he returned to Dayton to fetch his family—my Great Grandma Loretta and their three very young children: my great-uncle Chet, my great-aunt Florence, and my grandpa Lawrence.

J. E. Crosby family, 1908, photo from the author's family album]

Lloyd Atkinson, a long-time family friend, once recounted some early stories of making the acquaintance of my Great Grandpa Crosby. He explained how the Atkinson family assisted "Grandpa J.E." in various ways, and how Lloyd eventually wound up working on the farm. For many years, Lloyd and his wife, Mildred, attended nearly every Christmas Eve celebration as extended family. (I knew them as close friends, but never associated their relationship to my great grandfather with the heritage of our Michigan settlement. If I had realized they were so closely connected to Great Grandpa's business recovery, I would have asked a million questions.)

The details of Great Grandpa's family's new lives were not well documented, and little is known about where they first settled or how they survived. All we really do know is when their new prosperity began. In approximately 1913, Great Grandpa Crosby entered into a land contract to purchase some farm acreage that included two acres of peppermint. "Charles Sprague, who owned a farm near St. Johns in Clinton County, planted two acres of peppermint roots on his farm. The following year, J. E. Crosby, living just south of St. Johns, purchased the crop from Sprague and had the mint hay distilled about six miles northeast of Carson City in nearby Gratiot County. Other growers soon followed Crosby's lead."[5]

He learned how to harvest and process the precious peppermint oil and those two small acres grew into an almost-one hundred-year legacy.

Peppermint hauling, circa 1930s,
photo from the Crosby family album]

5 James Landing, *American Essence: A history of the peppermint and spearmint industry in the United States* (Kalamazoo, MI: Kalamazoo Public Museum Press, 1963), 85.

Many farmers followed his lead and the area of central Michigan became known as the "Mint Capital of the World." An article depicting the story of Grandpa J. E. was published on October 18, 1936, in the Lansing, Michigan, newspaper, *The State Journal* (twenty-two years after my great grandfather started his business). My uncle, Chet Crosby, was quoted in the article, saying "The market for peppermint oil is so limited that the increase in the number of growers has taken all but a very normal profit from the business. After we made a successful start, everyone thought he could get rich quickly by growing mint, and acreage soared."

As a pioneer of peppermint and spearmint farming, J. E. Crosby was a progressive grower. With the help of his two sons, Grandpa Lawrence and Uncle Chet, and later, his grandson (my uncle, Larry) and my father, J. E. Crosby revised the process of planting, harvesting, and transporting their crops. His heritage established our family footprint with the generations who have enjoyed his summer cottage and those who continue to drive past the old mint still to this day—in awe of the ambiance of the historic barn.

Eventually, my father had the entrepreneurial ambition to follow his father's and grandfather's example to purchase an exceptional farming operation that he "cultivated" into a fine business. He had the behavioral design—despite challenges and disappointments—to press onward to innovate, create, and maintain a thriving enterprise.

Although he was very adept at running a business, Dad's biggest challenge was sustaining our family throughout the winter months, as the farming revenues were not adequate to do so. Dad struggled to find ways to create supplemental income during those lean times. He tried selling real estate, but after a couple of bad breaks, he realized that he could not persevere through that type of uncertainty and pressure. He needed something more stable to provide for his family's security. Unbeknownst to him, he had some natural challenges—the same as anyone who has ever dealt with raising a family in a tough economy would.

First, Dad had two behavioral traits that contributed to his tactical challenge, and one external source that he did not understand how to respond to—his mother.

- Dad's mild-mannered, very low-dominance demeanor resulted in an internal struggle of how to implement the necessary calculated risks.
- Worrying would overwhelm him. Dad's high desire for conformity provided his adept ability to implement details, planning, and structures. But the other side of this cautious trait caused him to over-analyze and become anxious, which eventually absorbed any peace or optimism for his purpose.
- His mother, Grandma Esther, constantly discouraged him from buying or doing anything that she did not understand or approve of. No matter how hard he tried, she would admonish him by saying, "Oh, you cannot do that!" Sadly, after awhile, she was right. As a result of various misfortunes, he actually began to believe that success had eluded him—fearing it was available to others, but not to him. As for Grandma, I'll bet that she did what she thought was best, exercising her own cautious behavior while trying to be protective with his best interest in mind.

Did Dad have the behavior it took to be successful, or was a part of him just a dreamer? He obviously had something, because at twenty-one years old—married with a two-year-old child (yours truly)—he bought his farming operation. He did not need to be a "high dominant risk-taker;" his behavior needed to fit a "high patience," highly structured, extremely energetic profile to be successful.

Sadly, he never viewed himself as successful. Once seasonal farming activities were completed, the industry was a gamble. When unpredictable weather conditions crushed him, or some other unlucky episode caused him a loss of income, he always found a way to blame himself. Dad naturally lived with a fractured behavior, since his self-esteem was cracked due to self-condemnation.

Are there Core Behaviors a Person Needs as a Successful Entrepreneur?

Does being a successful entrepreneur require traditional risk-taking behavior traits, or can anyone with an idea and a deep passion become successful? Successful entrepreneurs, such as well-known moguls Warren Buffett, Bill Gates, and Steve Jobs—who have each implemented advances that have affected our society with their wealth and celebrity—seem to have a pronounced fascination within themselves.

History has shown us the formation of the small business enterprise. It is natural, when we think of the word "entrepreneur," to immediately identify anyone who either owns a business or who has started one. The dictionary describes an entrepreneur as "one who organizes and assumes the risk of a business or enterprise."[6] When we consider the essential traits of a successful entrepreneur, most of the focus is on attributes such as talent, experience, and education—the element of understanding one's temperament is regularly overlooked.

Any new businessperson is anxious when he or she is about to embark on a commitment, and making a risk-taking decision based on need and optimism. Typically the entrepreneur lacks the ability to assess thoroughly one's behavior, energy potentials, and style, as well as the role of the needed behavior to fill the position. While obvious criteria are defined in the job description, other important success factors are often missed because they are less understood and considered hard to measure.

---

6 Webster's New Explore Dictionary, Federal Street Press, Merriam-Webster, Incorporated, Springfield, MA, 1999

A common denominator in the entrepreneurial world is a risk taking behavior, and having clarity between "perceptions" versus reality. Confusion often presents itself in self-proclaimed entrepreneurs. Talented as promoters, they are able to visualize their product or process, and then they are able to sell and market it. However, they often struggle with adjusting to be more structured and patient to fill additional critical roles. They are almost always innovators, but sometimes fail when working with actual processes.

An Entrepreneur of the Times

Many economists consider the financial crisis of 2007–2008, also known as the "Global Financial Crisis" or "2008 Financial Crisis," to be the worst financial crisis since the Great Depression of the 1930s. Many people have found themselves unemployed—too young for retirement, yet too old to return to work. The shock and realization of a lost career seems like a bad dream requiring daunting change. This has triggered a surge of new entrepreneurs. For many, need has spurred risk-taking—people investing savings in the hope of reinventing themselves for self-employment.

The traditional process of creating your own business could include buying a franchise or leveraging a long-time hobby—the "American Dream" reinforced with ambition and undeniable risk. This is an opportunity for the entrepreneur today, due to the vast searching capabilities offered by the Internet. The world of Facebook, Twitter, YouTube, Google+, and other social networks populate the community, making the world a smaller place. There is a bold new frontier of possibilities on the Internet, offering twenty-four-hour unlimited potential. There has never been a faster way to create and maintain a social image worldwide. Today, people can market through social media without leaving the comfort of home. Someone who is passionate about sharing their story and knows the fundamentals of social media can create a niche that was never possible before now.

In the second grade, I refurbished my toys and sold the ones I had lost interest in by displaying them on a folding table near the street where there was high traffic and visibility. Every year I set up a lemonade stand, mowed lawns, shoveled snow, and performed services so I could buy hunting and fishing equipment or baseball gloves, and fix up my bike. Although I was of small stature, my heart was full, and hard work was built into my DNA. Imagine what I could have done if I had had the opportunities that young people have today.

Depending on the type of business you choose to pursue, my suggestion is to create a strategy based on function from every aspect of the job function, and then consider having a dual approach, i.e., two people who can offer the skills and behaviors to implement the whole package. Understandably, some business ideas do not need more than one person to execute. However, many business ventures need the complementary behaviors and talent of two or more people, so that the visionary can produce results, while the back room is being attended to, and the bills are paid on time.

A solo performer often has too many areas to focus on to be a well-rounded champion, because of this, outsourcing can be an option, but it is still not the complete answer. Every organization needs—and deserves—the proper behavior and talent. However, does the person who is about to risk everything really know himself or herself? If there is any apprehension about starting a new enterprise, that is the first warning that they should consider slowing down and reexamining their reasons for the new venture. Until they do understand themselves, they very possibly will experience the predictable pitfalls of lost time, lost money, and broken relationships.

The Mary Frances Shop

In the spring of 1967, during my first year of high school, my parents ventured into the world of retail clothing sales. In addition to their farming responsibilities, they opened "The Mary Frances Shop"—a women's clothing store that was to be managed by my mother, Mary. Their new business was born inside of an old, rented record store on Main Street in our hometown.

My mother, Mary Frances Crosby, was an attractive woman who was always well groomed and presented herself with a stately demeanor. She had a flair for fashion and an ease of interacting, so this business venture was a natural for her. Since she was always quite active in the community, this was an outlet she probably needed. The Mary Frances Shop was located just two doors down the street from the original location of Bruno's Restaurant (Grandpa's first business).

In reality, I would have preferred that they open a different sort of enterprise—perhaps selling men's clothing . . . or even pizza—but they opted for a women's shop. Somehow, this just was not very interesting to me. In fact, Mom also suggested to Dad that their business should be pizza, but he disliked the idea. A few years earlier, they had considered moving our young family to Wisconsin where they learned of a new restaurant craze that sold only pizza—years before the pizza franchise business became a billion-dollar industry. The bottom line is that Mom had the natural behavior to be successful with any business opportunity that she had a passion for—food service or fashion. However, she realized that she did not have the time that a restaurant would require, and the women's shop seemed to be a good fit.

Chapter Nugget

Entrepreneurs associated with successful accomplishments are popular, but until there is a comparison with greatness they seem to be people who are just driven with a cause. Traditionally people of difference are misunderstood for their talents and potential. What seems obvious is the importance to recognize what makes dreamer's dream—and to formulate a strategy to recognize their potential. The development of programs to recognize, educate and develop the inspiration of brilliance of young minds is essential for continuing to produce entrepreneurs, rather than discarding them because we do not understand them.

"If God gave me the choice of the whole planet or my little farm, I should certainly take my farm."
-- Ralph Waldo Emerson

CHAPTER 5

UNDERSTAND, ACCEPT, AND CELEBRATE

"How hard it is, sometimes, to trust the evidence of one's senses! How reluctantly the mind consents to reality."
-- Norman Douglas

Impacting Relationships

Consider the sacred place we all sometimes visit—our "room of deep mental orientation." This room contains our personal identity. It can be pleasantly illuminated, or kept in a dark and gloomy state. It might be a large room of fun and frivolity, or a closet of incarceration filled with depression, regret, and guilt.

I am not talking about mental illness; I am simply illustrating a place that may be familiar to most of us when we allow the outside influences of our successes and failures to define our behavioral uniqueness. I believe that "social craziness" resides in all of us to different degrees. When we apply the consequences of real-life circumstances, therein resides the "stuff" of the six o'clock news.

As we review our potential for happiness, we explore our desire to share our lives and experiences with a partner, unaware that our relationships eventually morph into something similar to a rollercoaster ride. When the spark of attraction ignites, our heart is set ablaze, the emotional "lever" is pulled, and life sometimes spins out of control. It is fascinating how we can be so surprised when differences and friction occur. Thinking that we bought a ticket to ride the merry-go-round, we are, instead, tipsy from a spin on the monster coaster. For some, this lifestyle is a turn-on—a necessary springboard for success and development. For others, it becomes a worrisome and anxious journey where the only thing we can be certain of is uncertainty.

While stoking the "fires of our desires" to achieve an exceptional relationship, our ability to understand comparative behaviors is critical. All of our good intentions will not adequately overcome the heartache of disappointment if we don't understand why our disappointments happen. When you understand the dynamics of similarities and differences in a relationship, you can actually have grace with the other person, knowing that they are not intentionally trying to hurt you.

Many people experience exceptional marriages by having failed ones behind them. If a survey were conducted of a population of happily married couples (and there is probably at least one out there), it is quite possible that the majority of those surveyed would admit to having a painful past, due to overreacting to problems or challenges in their relationship. Twenty years after my mother divorced my father, he still cried with regret that his pain was from his own stupidity, often due to overreacting to the little things Mom did naturally. He was angry with himself because his responses were exactly the opposite of what she needed to hear. She loved him, but his constant criticism and negative comments deeply wounded her.

For decades, too many relationships have come to disastrous ends. Our socially interactive culture has been plundered by the curse of divorce, and is in need of real solutions. What causes our precious relationships to implode? The fascinating component of attraction is that, typically, the very elements that draw two people together are the same dynamics that eventually tear them apart.

All through our lives, our relationships are an accumulation of personal interactions with one another. Human behavior provides the means for drawing people closer together or driving them apart. Communication styles eventually determine the outcome. Most often, our romantic tendency is to reminisce about how a relationship began, focusing on its uniqueness and intimacy, but, in reality, what is most important is how we finish—and that we finish strong.

Life is Quick

Somewhere I have a coffee cup that says I am fifty years old. Where did the last 12 years go? Not only is life short, but it is fast. It repositions itself like a young rabbit—hard to catch, and elusive. Our self-reflection from the innocence of childhood through generations of ancestors provides more wonder about "the why" we do what we do. For some families, life is blessed with achievement and accomplishment, but too many others have tragic memories of grief and pain caused by behavioral dysfunction. I recall helping a high school senior deal with his parents' failing marriage. One of his frustrations was with his father, who, for many years, read self-help books and even talked the "lingo"—yet, nothing ever changed—and his son wanted to know why. For many people, painful feelings of inadequacy contribute to flawed reasoning. Self-induced pain complicated by discord relating to a person's education, career, military service, marriage, or even travel contributes to feelings of emptiness.

During the Fall of 2005, being curious about how other people dealt with their behavior in their relationships and various circumstances, I launched a radio talk show called "Sound Behavior" on WLQV in Detroit, Michigan. The common denominator with so many of my radio show guests has been that they felt flawed. From college students to grandparents, damaged and blemished psyches are consistent. Our human inclination is to compare ourselves to everyone around us. With this type of appraisal logic, we can never achieve peace or true satisfaction. When someone makes a comment about our appearance or how we have changed, it can resonate to our "flawed" core and ignite the internal combustion of self-doubt and loathing.

Consider the types of questions that linger in the minds of many people: Did God have a rough weekend, and—on the morning of my birth—could He have made a mistake? Perhaps He just was not as alert as usual and really blew it with me. Am I such a "piece of work" that He broke the mold after my birth? Could this be possible? Picture this—you are lying on the table in the delivery room, and God throws up His hands in disgust and says, "I need to keep working on the prototype!" I don't think so!

The Holy Grail

Recall how, in the movie classic *Indiana Jones and the Last Crusade*, Harrison Ford—as Indiana Jones, renowned explorer and archaeologist—received a diary from his kidnapped father, Sean Connery. The document contained a lifetime of collected clues to map the possible location of the Holy Grail.

This epic adventure captures your imagination, which carries you on an action-packed and humorous journey in search of the Holy Grail. Once the cup is found—according to the movie—drinking from it produces eternal life. Imagine this possibility, and the thrill of discovering such a treasure. As competent adults, we can distinguish between fact and fiction; but there is that little child inside of each of us with hopes that say "what if?"

Consider the excitement of discovering the "Holy Grail" of ways of understanding people. How would you feel? Consider finding the key to unlocking the mystery of knowing yourself, your loved ones, your friends, and your coworkers. How would your life change?

There May be a Reason for our Inability to Understand

In general, we do not really understand others, and they have no clue about us. Even though we may have relationships, you can look into the eyes of your spouse, parent, sibling, friend, or anyone else, and know that she or he just does not understand you. To make things equally confusing, they may look into your eyes staring back at you, and become frustrated because they think you do not understand *them*.

From our heartfelt emotions, we express love, and because we love, we feel we should mindfully understand—and be understood. With love, understanding does follow as a by-product. But, just because we love does not mean this state of commitment provides clarity. Love and friendship do not permit us to discern what is going on in another's mind. Love provides us the grace to forgive, but in our minds, the offense distracts us and we become emotionally detached.

Perhaps our inability to understand others and ourselves is providential, as shown in chapter eleven of the book of Genesis. Genesis 11 is the story of the Tower of Babel. It tells the story of how people from all over the world came together to build an ideal city of the finest materials, with depth of design and glamour. They executed their plan that displayed their abilities and wisdom by trying to achieve greatness, and to prove it by building a tower so tall that it could be heavenly by reaching into the clouds. They had everything but humility, living in extreme competition to be the smartest and have the best (replacing their need for God) by building a tower that would reach to God.

The people in Genesis 11 accomplished their goals because, as verse one describes, they were in one language, and everyone understood one another. Imagine life without misunderstandings, arguments, or accusations. Genesis 11:1-9 describes how man dealt with pride and accomplishment and how God reacted to their accomplishments. "They were all in one language,"[7] and the Lord recognized that if man is able to easily communicate, then nothing is beyond their reach.

> 1 There was a time when the whole world spoke one language. Everyone used the same words.
>
> 2 Then people began to move from the East. They found a plain in the land of Babylonia and stayed there to live.
>
> 3 Then they said to each other, "Let's make some bricks of clay and bake them in the fire." Then they used these bricks as stones, and they used tar as mortar.
>
> 4 Then the people said, "Let's build ourselves a city and a tower that will reach to the sky. Then we will be famous. This will keep us together so that we will not be scattered all over the earth."
>
> 5 Then the Lord came down to see the city and the tower.
>
> 6 The Lord said, "These people all speak the same language. And I see that they all joined together to do this work. This is only the beginning of what they can do. Soon they will be able to do anything they want.
>
> 7 Let us go down and confuse their language. Then they will not understand each other."
>
> 8 So people stopped building the city, and the Lord scattered them all over the earth.
>
> 9 That is the place where the Lord confused the language of the whole world. That is why it is called Babel. And it was

---

7 Genesis 11:1, *Holy Bible: Easy-to-Read Version* (World Bible Translation Center, 2006).

> from there that the Lord caused the people to spread out to all the other places on earth.[8]

Consider the curse of confusion the Lord placed on the whole world in Genesis 11:9. Genesis 11:6 is profound in explaining that, when people communicate, they can accomplish anything they set out to do. Essentially, everyone struggles with communication. Moms, dads, brothers, sisters, and all other kinds of personal relationships are affected by miscommunication. Work groups with well-funded resources in all types of organizations have the same problems. People simply do not understand each other.

Naturally, mothers believe they understand their children. They may know what their child does—but they do not know why that child does it. Through their own perceptions, mothers may think they understand because they see similarities of their behavior in themselves, the father or other siblings, but in reality, they do not understand their child's behaviors or inherited traits. Mothers may believe that, because they gave birth to the child, they really know the child. The truth is that no one person really knows another. One may have a *perception* of another, but despite a deep love and good intentions, they may only have a friendship with—not a true understanding of—that person.

Some of the most challenging obstacles between people are those inadvertent offenses resulting from natural communication styles. Unfortunately, a person may negatively perceive and internalize comments or assertions of another due to their tonal expressions—in other words, not by "the what," but "the why." Thus, our natural response is to be offended and walk away, get angry, or maybe even exercise road rage. The most important thing to remember is: do not take it personally. Do not dislike the person; dislike the action. It sounds elementary, but often that simple action takes a village to sort out.

---

8 Genesis 11:1-9, *Holy Bible: Easy-to-Read Version* (World Bible Translation Center, 2006).

Trying to understand your loved ones should not have to be a long and complicated process. People are more complex than what our perceptions allow us to see on the surface. You simply need to remember that everyone has their own personal internal belief structure and some hold their rules to be absolute.

When our frustration turns into confusion and our patience has all but dwindled, we might be tempted to admit that we are never going to be able to understand our loved ones at all. We may feel confused because we think we should understand one another. When we do not—and are consequently tormented by the idea—we may reach destructive and catastrophic conclusions.

Do you think it is possible that everyone is walking in misunderstanding because of Genesis 11:9, where the Lord confused the language of the whole world? Consider what it would be like to understand the behavior of others. What would it mean to you as a mother or father if you could know why your teenager does what she or he does, so you would have a more meaningful approach to helping them? Is it really so hard to imagine?

Who would have ever thought you could send a letter instantly to anyone in the world—at no cost? Who would have ever believed you could share your photo album and so much more—with friends anywhere in the world? Who would have ever imagined that you could share "Tweets" and your whereabouts with anyone, anywhere, and at any given time? So . . . considering the endless possibilities of email, Facebook, and Twitter (just to name a few), who could ever have thought it possible to know another human being better than your mother knows you—in about six minutes?

What if there was a statistical process that would allow you to untangle these threads of confusion to understand "the why" you (and those around you) do what you do?

Breakthrough comes when you understand what you do, accept *why* you do it, and celebrate who you are. Depending on our roles in life, there are times when we need to make adjustments. We are all beautifully different, and those who seem to have it all, sometimes really do not. Remember that, as discussed previously, the primary obstacle preventing us to understand others is our own mind. For some reason, we naturally struggle—some, more than others—and our comprehension wrestles internally. However, it does not have to be that way.

Chapter Nugget

The process of maneuvering through life's daily challenges can be daunting. The key is to slow down and try to understand the entire situation before responding. Only then can the end goal be met with dignity and grace.

"Somehow, if you really attend to the real, it tells you everything."
-- Robert C. Pollock

SECTION TWO
PERFORMING IN OUR ROLES AND RESPONSIBILITIES

From the security of our homes, we begin to adjust our frame of mind from our personal environment to the energy of relationships, the workforce, educational settings, and a vast array of social settings. Chapters 6-9 link the diversity of personal experiences to the roles and responsibilities.

CHAPTER 6

THE REALITY OF ROMANCE AND MARRIAGE

"More marriages have been ruined by irritating habits than by unfaithfulness."
-- H. R. L. Sheppard

I will never forget the day when, as a little fellow, I walked past my parents' bedroom and noticed my mother sitting on the edge of the bed crying. With concern and curiosity, I entered the room and sat down to comfort her. As she dried her tears, she began to give me a little motherly advice. She said, "Someday, you will marry a special woman, and when you do, remember that she needs and deserves to hear how much you love her. Tell her how you feel about her, and compliment her on her appearance. I believe your father loves me, but I need him to tell me how he cares, and how much he appreciates me. But he never does!"

Looking back on Mom and Dad's life together, I can only imagine their loneliness. When they married, they were barely out of high school; Mom was only seventeen, and Dad, just twenty-one. Neither of them had a playbook for starting their new lives together. They moved from the romance of courtship—the balmy Sunday afternoons and dinners with the family, the anticipation of phone calls and post-cards—to the reality of daily life on the farm. The spark that ignited the fires of love and passion that brought them together was smoldering. By the time I came along, the honeymoon was over. They were moving apart and their issues were puzzling to them. Without having knowledge and understanding of their own behaviors and needs, how could they survive? However, they did, for twenty-eight years—with the same difficulties experienced by countless others. Going so far, yet missing the best years of their lives together, is a tragedy that far too often occurs to married couples.

Does my parents' story resonate with you? Historically, couples have had more information on how to assemble and service home appliances than they have had in successfully merging two lives. The phenomenon of two people enduring the obstacles of living together is not only a gamble, but remains a work in progress. The good news is that, because of the dysfunction and pain suffered by our ancestors, we are now able to uncover ways to help today's couples become smarter and more cohesive.

Really, how can we tout the brilliance of our new and improved ideas when the divorce rate continues to soar, resting at fifty percent? While our wonderful world evolves with sophisticated and wireless communications, flat-screen televisions, "smart" phones and fuel-efficient cars, countless couples are miserable and trying to hold on in hopes of survival—yet marriages are still failing.

My early apprehension toward marriage was, understandably, due to my parents' struggling relationship. Later, remembering when my own marriage was close to the three-year celebration and I was feeling some loneliness similar to my parents, I will never forget looking into my heart and asking what happened. What did I miss, or fail to deal with, when I felt the commitment of proposing to my sweetheart?

When was our honeymoon over, and what were the signs of this loving relationship slipping away?

I remember, on one short flight from Maui to Oahu, sitting on the plane with an emptiness in my stomach, feeling that our marriage was shipwrecked and we needed something special, or else it probably was not going to last. Quietly, I was praying: "Lord, what happened? What did I miss when experiencing my heartfelt emotion? Was getting married Your will, or my human desire?" Although it was not an audible voice, the quick response I heard in my heart was loud, clear, and unmistakable. "Nothing has changed," the Voice said. "Kathleen is the same woman you fell in love with, and she still loves the man she made her commitment to. Nothing has changed. Your own heart has turned, and you need to be more aware of her, her needs, your commitment, and the world around you—not how it seems, but what is real." From that moment on, my life began to change, as my heart had received an invitation to the start of a new outlook. I realized that it was up to me to grow up, man up, and become the husband with whom my precious wife deserved to spend the rest of her life.

One of my fondest memories as a husband came four years ago when Kathleen and I were on a business trip. I was speaking at a human resources conference for one of my larger clients. It was a Friday evening, and Kathleen and I were going out to dinner after checking into our hotel. From the start, Friday night has always been our "date night." One of my standards—and probably my smartest decision ever—was when I suggested to my new bride that we probably did not need the distraction of our friends and family to interfere with our Friday-night dates. This would help us focus on our relationship, the past few days, and what we had to look forward to during the week.

On this particular evening, Kathleen and I had just finished dinner and were waiting for our bill. Our server politely quipped, "I am sorry, I just have to ask you something. I, and all of the other servers, have been watching the two of you since you first walked in. The way you both look at and touch each other has convinced us that you must be newlyweds! Are you on your honeymoon?" I quickly answered, "Yes, we are!" After all, we were holding hands. The server said, "I knew it! When did you get married?" She was so excited by our obvious romantic behavior that I promptly and proudly responded, "In November, we will celebrate twenty-four years—and we are newlyweds because nothing has changed. Tonight is simply our date night."

Her demeanor immediately changed from the joy of what she perceived to be a newborn relationship to envy—as she began reflecting on her own less-romantic life. She and the others were smitten by the idea of a new romance in the restaurant, yet seemingly disappointed with reality.

I, however, am a happy man, deeply grateful for the riches received from my quiet conversation with God while flying over the Hawaiian Islands. He spoke to my heart to change our lives forever.

The Season of Single

Frequently, my radio show featured guests who were single people, bringing to light the topic of "behavioral fit." They all wanted to know what type of behavior in a potential mate would complement theirs, and wondered if this could be determined by comparing their ProScan assessments. Some of the guests were more comfortable with their unmarried status, while others were definitely interested in finding a life partner.

Being single can be either a comfortable, natural experience or an unhappy season of isolation and loneliness. Many singles go through life with a confident ease in their unattached lifestyles, while others are full of desire to find someone with whom to share their lives. Before searching for the ideal mate, there is priceless value to be gained by first discovering contentment within.

Too many singles set their sights on certain physical appearances and skip the importance of behavioral attributes in others, totally missing the opportunity to develop personal clarity in preparation to meet their soul mates. Social pressures, prejudices, and labels are somewhat responsible for the subconscious urgency to find a perfect match. Many singles turn away from social events feeling awkward, unfit, or somehow flawed because they do not have a partner or are not in a committed relationship.

The world of online dating is a constantly changing, ever-expanding, billion-dollar business because so many people are willing to search the world for the ideal companion. Whether you meet someone in the produce section of a favorite grocery store or while chatting online, it is important to understand behavior. Because entering into a committed relationship is life altering, it is important to keep your standards high and not settle for second best.

Prime Time

It is easy to find yourself suddenly single in the prime years of your life. Perhaps the consequences of infidelity, physical abuse, and financial stress or health issues have resulted in divorce. After a marriage fails, becoming single again is a daunting and painful experience. Surprisingly, everyday events like sharing meals and doing household tasks become missing routines while a feeling of relationship failure can contaminate your self-identity, giving way to damaged self-esteem and hopelessness.

A person's complete range of energy, decision-making style, and behavioral traits provide the predictability of how that person will confront the future and process the past. This is why self-behavioral clarity is priceless therapy. A relationship may have ended in perceived failure, but it does not have to destroy your personal identity. The value of self-image is critical to the ability to heal and rise above adversity.

No matter how deep the pain from a broken relationship or how long the season of brokenness, the ability to seek out and help someone less fortunate is a sure way to bring clarity after the pain. There is no such thing as a small act of kindness. To a homeless person, a fast-food bag lunch is as valuable as a fine dining experience would be to most of us. Yet, it is so easy to become numb to the needs of others while you are a victim of pain and loss. By accepting the challenge to channel your ambitions and energy to help the needy, it is possible to lose yourself in the process. Selflessly and frequently giving your time and talent to others will eventually replace your loneliness, emptiness, and pain with joy, happiness, and contentment.

It Could Happen to You

Reminiscing about my days as a single man brings to mind the comparisons of dating behaviors. My own ProScan assessment revealed an intuitive logic and high-thrust energy, describing me as an optimistic, reactionary person who made decisions quickly (although not carelessly), but often with little regard for the consequences. This is what is referred to as our "natural behavior."

When I was single, I was non-committal and lacked the appreciation of a rapport with a special person. Like many others, I was seeking pleasure—without the good sense or ability to maintain a long-term relationship. There were two providential experiences in 1981 that eventually contributed to the change in my values and my views on relationships. The first was a social invitation to visit the corporate headquarters of *Playboy* magazine in Los Angeles, California. Imagine having a front-row seat to observe the engine powering the machine of this fascinating empire and meet some exceptional people behind the scenes. The second was a visit to the Playboy Mansion with one of Hugh Hefner's personal photographers for a first-hand tour of the famed estate.

From this exceptional, once-in-a-lifetime experience came the subtle question that played repeatedly in my mind during quiet times: What type of life do I desire and with whom do I want to share it? This recurring question began to invade my thinking, and as time passed, it became louder.

Four years later, when Kathleen and I first met, the timing seemed inappropriate to begin a serious relationship. An attorney friend of mine introduced Kathleen to me as the paralegal who would be handling my corporate business transactions. After that first meeting in a professional setting, it was fascinating how frequently I began to notice Kathleen in restaurants in and around Lahaina town, even though we were also two very happily *unmarried* people.

From our very first date, there was chemistry that exposed our key behavioral similarities and blended our distinct differences into an effortless friendship. Even so, for me, the idea of marriage to Kathleen with her ten-year-old son was unimaginable, as I was experiencing serious stress from a business that was abruptly about to close. However, along with the fact that she was strikingly beautiful, something different became obvious to me. We enjoyed the simple facets of daily living, such as the same foods, the same music, running, working out, and a million other things that made our relationship easy and enjoyable.

Studying human behavior as a profession was indeed an auspicious path for me to follow because I remember being attracted to certain of her *behaviors* (as well as her physical beauty). Recognizing her high energy and instinctive natural ability for planning, she filled our activities with thoughtful details.

At the time, I was unaware of "the why" about Kathleen and me, but I could already sense major behavioral similarities that became entirely clear five years later, when we learned about ourselves through the results of our ProScan assessments. I'll never forget how we first glanced at the comparisons of our ProScan reports and had the ability to see on paper what we already knew, but suddenly saw with greater depth, value, and appreciation.

Our relationship developed by recognizing the essentials in our personalities and behaviors to help us overcome some of the distinct communication challenges that a new relationship presents.

The fairy tale begins when a man hopes his woman will never change, and the woman is sure that her man will *indeed* change, because he loves her. Kathleen and I don't live in a fairy tale, but we *do* live in a romantic comedy and just as it happened to us . . . maybe . . . if you know what to look for, it could happen to you.

Beyond Our Love

For years, many of my clients have contacted me with the question, "Don, do you think you can do for my marriage and family what you did for my company?" To my knowledge, in all of these cases, every opportunity that came our way provided life-changing improvements. Where separation and divorce had previously been imminent, it did not happen.

A few months before my father died, he and I had some time to talk. Out of nowhere, he shared something with me that nearly broke my heart. "When I married your mother," he said, "I just did not know that we were so different. I did not know how to communicate with her, or what she needed. Now, being around you, you have helped me to understand myself and my brothers, and the rest of the family. I think that if your mother and I would have had someone like you with your behavioral tool, perhaps our marriage could have been saved." For me, hearing this declaration from my father was heart stopping.

Fast-forward the story to six years later when my mother, Mary, came to visit for a couple of months. This was the first chance we had had to be together under one roof since I left home after high school graduation. We had a wonderful time reminiscing and savoring each priceless memory, but the day before she left, she shared something surprising. "Honey, you know that I have been a committed listener and supporter of your radio show and amazed at how you have helped so many people. After being a guest and listening to you on the phone, I finally understand. You have opened my eyes, and I have been thinking. Your father and I were so different; but I think if we had known someone like you, with your experience and intervention, maybe we could have saved our marriage."

As Mom shared her thoughts, she had no idea of the conversation I had shared with Dad, and inside my heart was an explosion of emotion. To this day, I ask myself the question, "To what degree am I to pursue the potential to help save relationships?"

Let me introduce you to the actual behavior of my mother and father so you can visualize some of their strengths and challenges by focusing only on the Dominance, Extroversion, Pace/Patience and Conformity traits.

First, as we have discussed, my mother is a highly extroverted person. She has an active ease of mixing with others, and is socially driven. She has a mild-mannered disposition with her low dominance and appreciates closure in all situations. She has some patience, but not has much as Dad's. She is exceptional with details (Conformity trait), and possesses high energy that enabled her entrepreneurial eagerness back in the days when she started the "Mary Frances Shop."

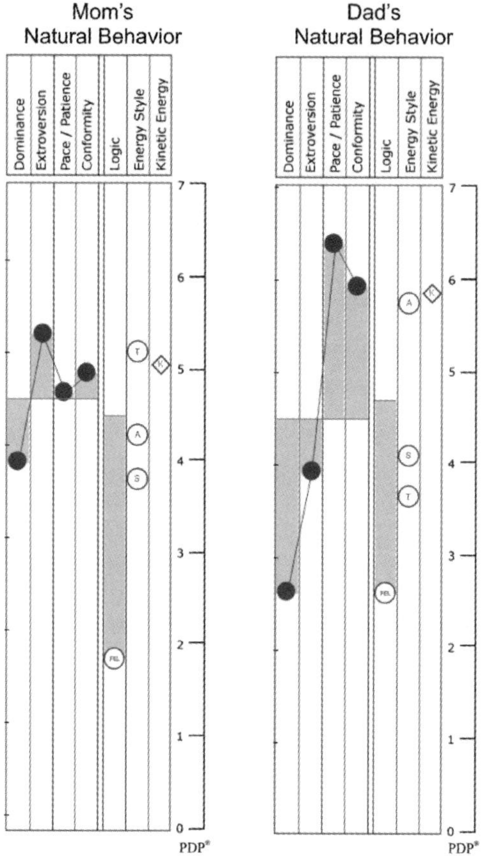

Dad was more mild-mannered than Mom and non-confronting because of his lower dominance. His strengths were evident by his intense need for everyone to follow his lead because of his high conformity trait. He, too, had an ease of interpersonal mixing, but a soft-selling communication style that did not really require the presence of others, unless they were family or close friends. With his high degree of patience, he was able to be an exceptional farmer and a good dancer, and quite adept at recognizing how things can come together for the common good. Dad had very high kinetic energy, which, combined with his high degree of patience and conformity, drove him to always undertake and successfully complete a large quantity of work.

If they could have understood their differences along with the similarities that drew them together, I believe my parents could have been a very happy and loving couple, successful in all aspects of their lives.

Personally I find it interesting where I have met individuals and couples who needed a touch of clarity and understanding to help them through their obstacles. We have met in grocery stores, standing in line at restaurants, at wedding receptions, baptisms, graduations, church, and on my radio show. Although my experience in helping families and couples is probably not a coincidence or an intentional act, my objective is always to help those who seem "just to appear." Maybe they are seeking that same enlightenment I experienced in Hawaii.

I was inspired by my father's relationship with my mother when I learned my father died still loving my mother even thirty years after their divorce from a twenty-eight year marriage. Obviously, love was not enough to hold their relationship together, thus creating the Beyond Our Love marriage program to help save marriages.

Many good marriage programs in the marketplace provide systematic guidance on how to stabilize a marriage. Beyond Our Love is neither a substitute for, nor does it compete with, any other marriage programs or counseling opportunities. Beyond Our Love is a practical application that provides couples with the necessary understanding that becomes the foundation to help take their relationship and marriage to the maximum level. Beyond Our Love is a weekend experience to rekindle a relationship involving a few hours on Friday evening and a half day on Saturday. The program was designed to be a safe progression of finding out and understanding why you and your spouse do what you do. Couples will learn how to get over hurdles and how to have a more accurate interpretation and awareness to better understand what is needed to save or empower their marriage.

Coffee with Grandma

My father's mother, Grandma Esther, knew I loved coffee with heavy milk and sugar. Some of my fondest memories of her are our "coffee conversations" in her living room next to her big picture window. She would rest in her favorite chair with me sitting across from her, while she did most of the talking. She asked me many questions, including: How was I doing? How were my parents? Then, without fail, she would probe to see if I knew what I wanted to do when I grew up. At first, I said, "No, Grandma, don't you know that I am only four?"

The continuum of her persistent questions about my future flowed throughout my adolescence. Soon, I thought I knew the answer. I told her that I was certain I was going to be a Detroit Tiger, and she said, "That sounds like fun—but I don't think so!" My eyes widened. "You can't do that," she said. "What do you *really* want to do?" I repeated myself, "I'm going to be a Detroit Tiger!" She went on. "Well, Don, you cannot do that, because you are going to work at General Motors." At that time, I did not have a clue what "General Motors" meant, but I was sure it did not have anything to do with a baseball team.

For the next couple of years, my future in a blue-and-white-striped baseball uniform with a large, cursive "D" on the jersey continued to fill my dreams and dominate our conversations. Eventually, due to my unfortunate series of accidents, my career in baseball began to fade like my favorite pair of jeans. Grandma Esther continued to ask, "Don, what are you going to do when you grow up?" My plans began to move in a different direction. I told her that I was going to travel to Alaska and California—to live in different states and have wonderful experiences. Again, she retorted, "Don you cannot do that!" Without hesitation, I insisted, "Yes I can, and I will!" She did not give up. "You cannot do that! You are going to live down the road from us, ride with your uncle, and go to work at General Motors."

Somehow, very early in life, I knew in my heart what I wanted to do, and I clung to my passion. Admittedly, at one point, I almost gave in to Grandma Esther's constant urging. After graduating from high school, I considered working on the line at GM for the summer. Again, she had her own ideas. "Oh, NO, if we are going to ask your uncles to use their influence to get you a job, you are not going to make it temporary; you are going to make General Motors your life!" Her demands made it easy for me to walk away. The decision of whether or not to make a career at the automobile plant took about three seconds. I felt—and still feel—no ill will toward GM. It is a fine company and a great place to work for many people—just not for me. If only Grandma and the rest of my family had really known me, maybe they would have understood the depths of what I needed to do.

Your Annual Snapshot

Step outside the boundaries of your reality and consider your design. Consider the possibility of statistically recording and tracking your behaviors. Imagine, from birth, your parents expecting to learn of your behavioral distinction on your tenth birthday. From this date forward, each year, they are going to review your behavior and measure it scientifically. As parents, they are going to have a snapshot of who you are, and as your relationship with your parents matures, there will be less friction and frustration for everyone. With age, your relationship will more easily grow into oneness, and many of the challenges that naturally occur within families (like between my father and me), will be greatly reduced, if not eliminated altogether.

Each year, they will monitor your stress level with a nurturing style. They will talk with you to find out where your stress might be coming from, so you both can understand how you feel. Then, they will discuss with you the possibility that perhaps you are trying to mirror the temperament of a loved one or someone you simply admire. Through this process, they are going to have direction in how to communicate with you and support your needs as you mature. When you struggle with sports, cheerleading, or chess club, they are going to know how to help you. When you are down, they will have the ability to support you, and, emotionally, you will have a greater level of acceptance. Hopefully, your stress level will diminish.

You will be able to reestablish the love you have as a family by the way each of you will get along. As you contemplate continuing education or an industrial career path, your parents, grandparents, or guardians will have more clarity with you and your decision, rather than their own ideas of what they feel will be good for you. As you eventually meet the person who fills your soul—who has had the same coaching while growing up—you will be able to understand one another's behaviors and how you compare as a couple.

From Age Ten, to College, and Marriage

Very close to his tenth birthday, my nephew, Kevin, participated in his first ProScan behavioral survey. From that moment on, we bonded on a dynamic, new level. Even as he was coming of age, he realized how deeply I came to know him through the accuracy of the survey. Thus began a sweet, cohesive, friendship, like father and son.

The power of knowledge and the ability to apply wisdom is truly priceless. I recall talking with him on the phone when he was in college and I could hear the excitement in his voice. He had a girlfriend, and asked, "Uncle Don, could we do a survey on her to see if we are a match, and whether we could get along?" Subsequently, during seasonal breaks, they traveled to Michigan from Pittsburgh, Pennsylvania, to discuss and compare their assessments. As bright, young, adults they received the information openly, and following my interpretation. In time, they embraced the truth and eventually walked away from the romantic relationship as friends.

Later, on one special occasion, Kevin asked if we could do another survey. "Uncle Don," he implored, "She is the one—I can just feel that she is the right woman for me. Can we do a survey to confirm how I feel?" We indeed surveyed Liz, and she happened to be an exceptional complement to him. Today, they are a beautiful couple, successfully developing, yet eliminating the drama and heartache that too many couples endure. Recently, they welcomed their first child, and celebrated her baptism.

During times when technology is moving faster than you can assimilate, imagine yourself having the ability to understand your family. There is significance in the passage of time, and the reality of living life from ten years of age to becoming a father happens within the blink of an eye.

While staying with my family on one of my last nights in Michigan before moving to Alaska, I wrote the poem following the Chapter Nugget. At the time, my younger brother, Jimmy, was only eight. I was twenty-two, and this was the last time I was home before my parents' divorce.

Chapter Nugget

In every relationship, challenges are a natural occurrence. Even those who are the closest to their partners and have the fewest issues will struggle from time to time. The wisest strategy is to try to understand the *fit* before you *commit.* Too many people avoid this process for fear of discovering something negative, rather than learning how to adjust. Invest in your future by finding out how to make your loving relationship work.

His Child

The beauty of a child is innocence.
A straight answer or an honest question;
No cheap replies but a soft reason why.
When his mind expands
And his body grows,
The time has come when it is his child
That wants to know.

CHAPTER 7

BEHAVIOR IN THE WORKPLACE

"When love and skill work together,
expect a masterpiece."
-- John Ruskin

Help Wanted

Have you ever entered a restaurant and been disillusioned because no one seemed to be on shift? You waited patiently for your table, waited again to order your meal, and finally, the food arrived. Oh, by the way did you happen to notice the "Help Wanted" sign in the window? You did, and still you went in, expecting a five-star experience.

The need for convenience fills our lives, and, for that, a strong, well-trained workforce is critical. Regardless of the type of service, we, the consumers, expect—and delight ourselves in—the amenities of polite and personal attention more than ever.

For the employer experiencing the "people" side of the business, attracting and creating a successful employment base might be compared to rolling the dice at your local casino. The common denominator is the anticipation of hitting the jackpot—despite the high stakes of probable loss.

Organizational Repair and Maintenance

As companies identify their need for selecting a standardized hiring program, they become acutely aware of their need to stabilize the current work environment. The Organizational Repair and Maintenance concept (ORM) is—for your company—akin to the maintenance schedule of an automobile.

When you take possession of your vehicle, the automobile has maintenance requirements. The more miles you drive your car, the wider the variety of preventive maintenance procedures. You make an appointment to change the oil, check all the fluids, and rotate the tires. As the service writer greets you, before he logs your auto into their system, he asks you what the problem is, the reason for the visit, and how your vehicle is performing. He documents everything you recognize as "immediate need," and you share your impression of how it is running. He listens to your story and documents the service ticket. The technician drives your vehicle into the stall and the first function is to plug it into the diagnostic computer to learn its condition.

Your follow-up with the dealer or repair shop addresses everything you knew needed attention, in addition to other issues that will need care now or sometime in the near future, and an estimate of costs to cover the work.

In most companies, everyone is so busy with meetings, projects, and daily distractions—while still trying to maintain, stabilize, and grow the business—that we somehow do not always find the time or energy to think beyond our critical functions. The consequence of this is comparable to driving your vehicle two hundred thousand, three hundred thousand, or even six hundred thousand miles on the same set of tires without an alignment or the proper maintenance. Suddenly, with our company-wide "service record" being poor to non-existent, we wonder why our organization is not running well.

Each company—instead of waiting for the tires to come off—needs to develop a strategy with a starting point directed to its immediate needs. Next is the task of implementing a diagnostic process of understanding and developing the current staff, and establishing a standardized hiring system to reduce employee turnover.

If a business has more than one employee, there is a high probability that the company will experience behavioral challenges within the workforce. Through the years, I have heard outrageous complaints from business owners, managers, board members, CFOs, and CEOs. The situations they described would easily influence any employee to keep his or her dreams of advancement a secret.

When working with leaders of these organizations, one of the most common questions I have been asked is, "Have you ever worked with another company in our industry?" I will answer that question with a question: "Do you really think that the root of your industry challenges is isolated to your industry?" Actually, the situation is more often a people problem packaged in an "industry challenge" wrapper.

Here are just a few short stories of leaders who have experienced situations that may be similar to yours.

The Struggles of Manufacturing

When I first met the human resources manager, I was assisting the company's leadership team during the transition process after their manufacturing plant was first sold to a public company. Almost two years to the day, that HR manager was calling me again to schedule a meeting. The call was an invitation to return to discuss the possibilities of helping them with their latest compelling difficulties. Employee morale was horrible, but this was only one of many other challenging issues facing this eighty-five-year-old company.

A few minutes into our conversation at the plant, the general manager offered a "walk-through" introduction. As soon as we stepped onto the pathway toward the team in the first machine area, the hair on the back of my neck stood up. During our introductions, their expressions and attitudes were most interesting. Although I was a guest, their smirks of anger were not well hidden behind their smiles. When we returned to the general manager's office, he asked me what I thought.

"Well, you have a choice," I said. "You can move your equipment to another location and turn this plant into an antique mall. Or, we can hit it head on and assess your entire organization. We can implement a culture of clarity and understanding and try to get a breakthrough to help everyone who still likes and appreciates their positions here."

During our team sessions, the common denominator was that each cell group happened to have two or three people whose bitterness influenced the others by stirring up ongoing dissensions. I began our meetings by offering them a choice: they could stay and work with us, or—if they were so tired of their positions and hated being there—they were free to leave. We let the employees know that the company was finished with abrasive opposition, and had scheduled group interviews with two outside companies for anyone who wanted to transfer. We told them that, on the next Saturday from ten o'clock in the morning until two o'clock in the afternoon, there were going to be interviews with a major fast-food chain and a mass-merchandising retail store for their transition.

When I held up the job application forms to be passed around, the production manager shot me a glare that questioned my motives and sanity. What was I doing? One could only imagine the incredible silence that followed.

As the workers grumbled, I said, "Okay, if you are going to feel so sorry for yourselves, we are going to take a short field trip. We are going to visit the child burn center to see what having a bad day really looks like, and on the way back, we will stop by the nursing home so you can compare your empty positions here at the company with a life spent playing cards and searching for lost memories. Today, you have the ability to do something different. But, if you are going to stay here, there will be a resolution to change attitudes. Let us fix the issues that have been bothersome for too long and improve working conditions. Life is too short."

The rhythm of the room changed from an increasing roar of anxiety and anger to one of total disarmament. The quietness that melded all those people together was irreplaceable as each person was mentally on that field trip. They quickly understood the circumstances of those whom we would be visiting, and came to realize that their own challenges paled by comparison. For a while, the threat of that field trip created the framework for implementing a new foundation for progress.

Working in conjunction with the Human Resource Manager we completed team sessions for every group within the plant, one-hundred and ninety workers participated and the return on the company's investment was exceptional:

- The overall morale of the plant improved and a large number of the workers became less pressured and more appreciative.
- Together, with the management team we established new employment processes and, from these, the company received a reduction of seasonal employee turnover by forty percent—a savings of approximately fifty-eight thousand dollars.

- Production increased in one particular assembly line by two percentage points, which was equivalent to making an increased profit of two hundred and fifty-six thousand dollars in just eighteen months from the date of our case study.

The exceptional financial return came while working with one particular team of eleven staff members. This group was all cross trained so moving people on the production line was not an issue. After reviewing the ProScan data sheet graphs of two production line workers, in particular the lead person and the last person, a "red flag" had emerged. The lead person had an "achiever" energy capacity, which is very effective for maintaining production. The very last person on the line had an "ultra force high achiever" capacity, which is ideal for picking up the urgency and tightening up the slack. My suggestion was to swap the positions of these two people, by moving the lead person from the front of the line to the back, and vice versa. The suggestion worked, and as far as I know, is still working today.

The bottom line for that company was an improved workforce, a one hundred fifty-eight-thousand-dollar savings in eighteen months, and an ongoing profit—all because of an improved assembly process.

Traditional Healthcare

Through a variety of opportunities, I have had the pleasure of assessing the behavior of many doctors and nurses. Because of the increasing regulations and changes in this industry, it is critical that leadership understands the organization's behavior, how to leverage talent, improve communications, and reduce conflict. I will never forget a project where a large hospital contacted me to participate in their family practice retreat.

Even at a retreat, all of my sessions include the participants completing our ProScan assessment, where I introduce people to themselves and their colleagues from a position of authenticity as well as perception. One of the priceless benefits ProScan is that it affords me, as a facilitator, the ability to understand my audience and the ability to disarm almost any behavioral challenge.

During the week before the retreat, I visited the hospital, followed and chased down twenty-eight doctors between their rounds to debrief them with their profile results. I was very impressed by the incredible pace of their schedules and the volume, variety, and intensity of their activities. The real challenge began as we came together for our one-day group meeting at a local conference center where I was about to earn my fee.

With my PowerPoint presentation, I presented the basics of the PDP. As I eased into introducing the doctors to themselves and to their colleagues, I was about halfway through the third introduction when one of the doctors raised his hand and said, "I would like us to vote, either to stay here and waste our time, or leave like we did yesterday and go back to work." I wondered what he meant by that statement. I was not informed if he had done the same thing the previous day, stopping the first day of their two-day retreat. I was blindsided by his statement and wondered why he had made it.

With a quick glance around the room, I turned to assess the composure of the doctor in charge of the group's general practice. I immediately felt his expression of defeat. About twenty seconds had passed, and I interrupted the situation to regain control of the audience by confronting the doctor who had raised the question. I said, "Thank you for your sincere expression of how you feel, but we just began this session. Are you willing to miss a potentially life-changing day because of your impatience?"

From there, I moved the introduction from the third doctor to my new, outspoken friend, and I began to introduce him to his colleagues explaining why he was so outspoken and felt that his opinion was the only one that mattered. My introduction professionally dissected his behavior, turning him from being outspoken to speechless, and I shared this with his colleagues. "This, ladies and gentlemen, is why he does what he does. You just have to know him, understand him, and forgive him for his abrasive behavior."

Suddenly, the most beautiful thing happened. The doctors began to open up and share their feelings about this outspoken doctor and his unorthodox control. One of them was eight months pregnant and started to cry, describing his rude and unprofessional behavior. I proceeded continuing on with the introductions for the next forty minutes. When we were breaking for lunch, the executive director thanked me for the professional outcome and shared that he could now relax, knowing that the day had already been successful. However, he felt the success of our session was going to continue to make a priceless impression on their family practice and improve their professional relationships.

Here is where the brilliance of academia meets the passion of the heart. Without concession, people—regardless of their roles—make a valued contribution to the outcome of the exceptional patient experience. The entire industry deserves the results of synchronized communication resulting from understanding behaviors and practicing professional courtesy.

Intuition and the Cost of Hiring

Have you ever listened to an interview between sports commentators and coaches discussing their team strategy to overcome their opposition? The on-screen interview goes something like this: "So, Coach, what will be the turning point between you and this outstanding competition?" The response frequently is described in one word: turnovers.

"We need to hold on to the ball to control the game. If we do not throw the ball away, we can dominate with our offensive game and wear them down with the penetration of our defense."

Traditionally, coaches and sports professionals teach about the repercussions of making errors and analyze the cost of errors. Dropping the ball, striking out, running over the base, and stripping the ball from the running back are errors that will create a negative momentum and contribute to the probability of losing the game. When a team provokes a penalty, the chances of winning are reduced and the team has to work extra hard to recover from the physical and mental exhaustion.

Even though the concept of turnover is understood in sports, it is not trusted in business because of human issues and industry standards. Instead of paying attention to what is going on around us, as "Monday morning quarterbacks," we come into our offices and learn from our accountants that our business is experiencing employee turnover exceeding thirty percent.

During one beautiful fall afternoon, I received a telephone call from John, the owner of several high-end restaurants in Hawaii. His company had been a client of mine for a couple of years, but he wanted to ask my opinion of an important strategy he was contemplating implementing. He explained that he was thinking about hiring a particular executive chef from New York City and, because the investment would be substantial, he was interested in my insight from the applicant's ProScan assessment. After a couple of minutes, I said, "You recognize that is inappropriate for me to suggest what choice you should make. But I will provide you with an understanding of his behavior and what might happen if you move him across the country and add him to your organization."

One of my concerns was that the applicant's behavior was so similar to John's that there could easily have been friction between the two headstrong men. In my estimation, it would not be long before the applicant would attempt to take control, if he were not given it in the first place. This was among several of my apprehensions as John and I discussed his plans for this acclaimed culinary rock star. Obviously, this was not what he wanted to hear and I wondered what he would decide. Although, because I already knew John's profile, I knew that he would hire his applicant.

Approximately six months had passed when I received another call from John wondering when my schedule would be bringing me back to Oahu. I could not resist asking if he made his hire or if he, in fact, had walked away. Sheepishly, he shared that his decision had been to hire the executive chef—and he admitted that everything I predicted had become a reality. He conceded that, as our initial phone conversation replayed in his head, he kicked himself for the expensive distraction he would never forget.

During a workforce development session with his leadership team, he announced that if he had listened to the content of our phone conversation, rather than only hearing what he wanted to hear, he would have saved himself about one hundred and fifty thousand dollars.

How many employees can a company afford to hire for the entry level, manager, and executive players before it is time to close the doors to unanticipated overhead costs? Being a Monday morning quarterback with the hiring process is getting into the game a day too late. Sometimes our natural behaviors are so strong that for us to adjust ourselves from what we want to do to what we know we *should* do is our greatest challenge.

A School District Hiring through the Traditional Process

When he first started working with the Michigan Association of School Boards (MASB), the current head of superintendent search, Dr. Carl Hartman, identified a search that would be an exceptional pilot program, but he needed help to provide superior service for the school district. A few days later, I drove to Upper Michigan to attend the school's board meeting to introduce our new program to the board. Included in my introduction was my invitation for the board members to experience a ProScan assessment so I could demonstrate the process and the value of the service we were going to provide.

Next, we created a specific job model which measured the ideal behaviors for this open superintendent position. The board reviewed and approved the model and we began moving forward. The volume of applications Dr. Hartman collected was impressive and, within a short time, he had thirty-three highly qualified applicants complete a ProScan survey to cycle through the school board's interview process. MASB coordinated the school board members so that they could interview all thirty-three applicants not once, but three times each. They completed ninety-nine interviews during this exhausting process. Once the board made their selection, Carl called and asked me who, out of the thirty-three applicants, was my top pick. When I told him, he almost fell out of his chair before he asked me how I knew.

Our applicant ranking report had statistically listed the group of applicants, and the highest-ranking person happened to be the same applicant the board had handpicked after their grueling interview process. The only difference was that our method was faster and very scientific, demonstrating that any organization could eliminate the traditional hiring process, if it could be receptive to changing its method for doing so.

To launch their new relationship between the school board and the new superintendent, I attended a board meeting where I introduced the new superintendent to each school board member, and each of them to him. That evening, we eliminated the learning curve of each of their relationships and they began to interact with clarity. From the perception of everyone involved, the hiring process for the school district, the new superintendent, and the Michigan Association of School Boards was priceless.

Construction Signs Are Intended to Protect You

In construction, communication is imperative and trust is essential. By slowing down from emotional reactions long enough, you will able to make the appropriate decisions by reading the signs around you. The following story is about someone I have worked with in that business.

When Brian called, he was angry, frustrated, and torn between his emotions and his responsibility of managing his workforce. He asked, "Don, what do I do? I have known Ken for years; we have shared many similar experiences growing the business. Our families have been friends for a long time, and I like him. But I cannot have him work for me any longer. He's done. I am so angry I just want to scream!" I listened until he repeated, "Don, what do I do?"

Even though firing Ken would have brought Brian the emotional satisfaction of doing what he believed he should do in that moment, the decision would only have resulted in a short-term relief. Ken's performance and potential—and their years of friendship—presented a challenge for how Brian was going to discipline his manager.

My suggestion was: "Brian, you have probably said and done all you or anyone else could do, but let us try one more idea. Consider us meeting in Houston for a couple of days and let me figure out if I can reach him. If it is possible to accomplish my mission with Ken, maybe I will have time to review the hiring process to see if I can help identify why employee turnover is so unusually high with the laborer position in your company."

A couple of weeks later, I went to Houston, where Ken and I worked through a three-hour lunch, discussing his natural tendencies. His moment of revelation came when he learned that his abrasive demeanor—although unintentional—was damaging his relationships with the very people he cared about most. When we met, however, he knew that his career was on the line and that he had better listen to me and figure out how he was going to move forward—with or without the company. The choice was his.

This type of "stay-or-go" situation has a tendency to spark a sensitive note and cause a reaction of resistance, anger, and rejection. What I was aiming for with Ken was his mature acceptance of responsibility by asking Brian and his managers for forgiveness, and—with a new commitment for improvement—for him to become the branch manager Brian had hoped he could be. I knew he had the potential; I could see the regret in his eyes and hear the brokenness in his voice.

The good news is that Ken received the advice. His rough attitude changed into a willingness to do the necessary things to repair his standing within the company. After lunch was our team session with Ken's group. During our team session, he described some of the moments of our one-on-one meeting and he apologized for being a part of their stress. He called Brian and humbly thanked him for his confidence and investment in him by giving him the opportunity to work with me.

The next step for Brian and me was to determine why their company's turnover was so high. After reviewing the behavioral charts of every new hire, termination, or current employee in the field maintenance position for the last six to eight months, I learned that the company had been hiring a large population of social extroverts—the opposite type of behavior proven for this job position.

The company's propensity to hire this type of individual puzzled me. Their presumably sharp manager always knew where he could find men that needed work. This strategy would ordinarily have certain benefits—one that would make him seem like a star recruiter. His lifestyle of visiting bars and shooting pool with his peers after work was his plan of finding workers.

Thus, he would go to the bar to socialize and, at the same time, find out who needed money and who was interested in working. The next day, the new recruits would arrive to accept their promised opportunity, and work the exhausting daily routine of the field maintenance position until they tired of manual labor in the hot sun. This scenario kept repeating itself.

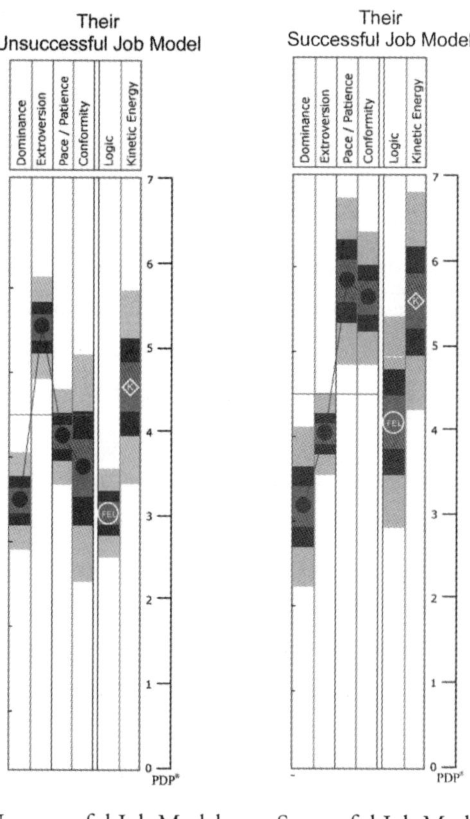

Unsuccessful Job Model specific only to this aforementioned company.

Successful Job Model specific only to this aforementioned company.

Before departing Houston to return home, I facilitated the creation of a successful job model for the field maintenance position, using the people who had been successful in the position along with those considered as exceptional workers from other divisions. I showed the branch manager the ease of working with their PDPWorks program, and left there exhausted—and a full two days behind schedule.

The following incalculable results emerged:

- Brian and Ken restored their relationship and continued to develop improved communications.
- Ken grew into a higher level of responsibility with his employer.
- As a producer, Ken's construction project sales increased, but with less friction.
- The laborer position employee turnover practically stopped, the company saved a significant amount of money, and the frustration level diminished.
- Morale improved with the other managers.
- My relationship with Ken, Brian and his company has thrived and some solid friendships have formed.

Brian's decision to take the extra step by asking for help demonstrated exceptional leadership. Had he kept his frustrations to himself, the outcome would have been very different.

Chapter Nugget

While recruiting for new hires, companies traditionally try to identify the right attitudes, the right accomplishments, and the right experience to fit their needs. However, when employees fail, it is usually due to behavior-related circumstances. Learn why some of your employees are more successful than others in the same job position. Then consider replacing the gut feeling method of hiring and managing people with a proven scientific process, stop gambling with your company's future.

"If you have more than one person in any relationship, you have behavioral challenges."

CHAPTER 8

IT IS ALL ABOUT THE STUDENTS

"What is learned in high school, or for that matter anywhere at all, depends far less on what is taught than on what one actually experiences in the place."
-- Edgar Z. Friedenberg

The Innocence of Children

While I was sitting on the porch of my small, but lovely home in Ashland, Oregon, on one particularly beautiful morning during the spring of 1980, a group of approximately thirty visiting angels touched my heart.

I had just lost my job as crew leader/closer of one of two sales teams for the local car dealership, Bob Frink Chevrolet. As a young man of twenty-five years of age, that job had been a perfect fit for my personality and lifestyle. I deserved to be dismissed because my priorities had been out of order, and there was no one to blame but myself. The owners and senior managers of the dealership were good men to whom I remain grateful for having given me an opportunity. I solely owned the failure, the disappointment, and uncertainty that were now a part of my future.

Earlier that spring morning I had taken a scenic run through the hills of my neighborhood and performed my usual weight lifting routine. That was how I chose to begin each day, but due to the uneasiness in my soul, the day felt different. Therefore, when I arrived home, I pulled my rattan rocking chair from the living room to the porch, positioned my Bose speakers at the two rear corners of the porch, and cranked up the volume. While sipping a large tumbler of vodka and orange juice, I hoped the music and alcohol would deaden the pain.

While settling into my reverie, I watched Romeo, my beautifully groomed American Cocker Spaniel, playfully take care of his own exercise routine by running across the front lawn. Romeo scampered excitedly as a large group of school children with Down's syndrome approached him on the sidewalk. These beautiful children, without a care in the world, were frolicking, skipping, and running alongside Romeo. Their laughter evoked the puppy inside my mature dog and deeply touched my heart. There, in that brief moment, the intense happiness, sweetness, and love that poured out to Romeo from those thirty children was mesmerizing. As I glanced at the new car and boat in my driveway, I realized what the children would never be able to attain or experience. How starkly their lives contrasted to mine. This was a virtuous experience as I became intensely embarrassed by my gross self-absorption. I sat there wishing that I could freeze the moment in time and that those precious children would never leave.

Eventually, Romeo tired of all the excitement and returned to the porch, settling down beside me, as the children continued on their way. When the last child was almost out of sight, I pulled the plug on the stereo, moved everything back into the house, and dumped my cocktail into the sink. Fortunately, my sense of perspective had been heightened before the alcohol had had a chance to dull the moment. The lesson was that I needed to take my eyes off myself, step back, and evaluate the problem. My unemployment was just a speed bump of distress among the many pieces in life's puzzle—more of an inconvenience than a problem. As I continued to deal with my personal crisis, I sensed that the appearance of that beautiful band of visiting angels was not just a coincidence.

The impact that those children made on me in 1980 was a powerful antidote to my brokenness, revealing a clear view of my personal delimiters. This experience is as powerful to me today as it was then, and helped me to move my life from the front yard to the classroom.

The Heart of Teaching

The profession of "educator" has historically attracted people with a special combination of behavior and talent from the labor force. Traditionally, those who are able to build a foundation of understanding and encouragement largely filled the role of "teacher," while also providing their students a safe haven from reality through learning and imagination. Many stories describe how just one teacher who believed in a particular student made the difference to help that child become unusually successful. Teachers who guide young and impressionable children are the superheroes of our society affecting future generations. These incredible educators typically received their gratification through the success and well-being of their students.

Capturing the Missing Potential in Our Children

Customarily, the natural, social behavior of students has guided educators to predict the percentage of who would, and who would not, make the grade. A child's performance and his interaction with his teacher were clues to the outcome of that students learning experience.

Students basic needs could be met and their lives would be relatively uncomplicated if they tested well. The odds would be in their favor for success. However, the academically, socially, and economically less fortunate simply have to work harder to survive.

Many of the challenges in today's educational system have been in existence for quite some time. Classically, we identify students of exceptional achievement as "shining stars;" we define the average population as the status quo "nice kids" who blend in without drama, while the below-average performers are the low percentile on the bell curve, the "strugglers". With those groups in mind, teachers approaching their new school year observed how students would rank in their overall class population, and expected that not all would make the grade.

How can we further help the struggling students who desire to climb to the top of their class?

Many students struggle with learning for a variety of reasons, and often understanding their natural behaviors can identify these challenges. It is even much easier to teach students who have a learning disability when these behaviors are understood.

For example:

- The dominant person generally understands quickly, but naturally struggles mentally and can become bored from a traditional slower-paced teaching style.
- The predictable extrovert can be easily distracted by everything around them.
- While the patient students will quietly think about everything…and struggle with closure.
- The conformity students may be extra hard on themselves bringing anxiety into situations.

Consider these variables by combining them together into trait patterns where one person may have several of these temperaments and the outcome can seem complicated and overwhelming.

Other learning challenges are presented, such as speaking in front of the class and testing. Some students find it hard to get up in front of others, and some just do not test well under pressure. In both cases, these students can—and too often do—fall through the cracks.

Now, more than ever, young people simply want others to understand them. Students everywhere are acting out in reaction to their pain. In the past, we seldom heard of the tragic incidents that are occurring in small towns today. Now, all too frequently, this has permeated our communities.

The New ABCs of Education

Consider the assumptions made by the concept of the "bell curve" probability theory in anticipation of the new school year and which students will succeed. Simply put, history reveals that not all students will excel - a percentage of them will be at the top of their class, others will struggle with failing grades, while the largest group will fall in the middle. Consider what would happen if we eliminated and substituted a theory with openly focused attention on the students' "Attitudes," learning about their personal "Behaviors," and providing them with a "Curriculum" through an enhanced communication learning style. Through the alignment of the new ABCs of Attitude, Behavior, and Curriculum, a teacher will not need the entire year, but rather, just a few days, to get to know the students. The purpose is to eliminate feeling you know someone, by having behavioral specifics, which should improve student grade point averages and improve the learning experience of the student.

Teaching anyone with a negative attitude is exhausting. When a person with a bad attitude is unwilling to learn and is otherwise distracted, his defiance is exacerbated. This can affect an entire classroom, flowing out like ripples in a small pond. How do we effectively teach students who have negative attitudes? The challenge is difficult at best.

Imagine being a teacher and, every day, having to face a semi-hostile environment. The continual energy drain would smother your career dreams as each day turns into a fight for survival.

When we consider the high dropout ratio of students—as well as those who barely graduate—we realize that we have a large population who will struggle in need of two jobs rather than one. Owning a home and driving a new car might be only a dream unless they have parents or relatives to help.

What if teachers and parents could actually understand each student and his or her behavior during the first week of the new school year, rather than after it has ended?

Special-Needs Students Excelled When They Were Understood

Why should children have to internalize pain when they sense that they are below-average learners? How must they feel when they begin to stand out in the class because they seem to be not as smart as the rest? Sadly, often these students fail to recognize their unique abilities and worth. Mainly, because they learn differently, they do not accept themselves, and they feel "damaged." As the downward spiral continues, they are likely to transfer from a "standard" classroom to an alternative education environment, losing the experience of being with the other kids as their struggles continue.

As students move to the playground to choose teams based on athletic prowess, consider the feelings of the students who are the last chosen, or not chosen at all.

Through my experience working with school superintendents, their boards, and other educators, a Ph.D. was unnecessary to discern the pain that exists in our educational system. Seeing a snapshot and hearing of an epidemic fueled by bullying, teen pregnancies, a high dropout rate, drug overdoses, and suicides was enough to make me examine opportunities for improvement.

I was anxious to test drive and transfer my proven methods from the twenty plus years in the corporate setting to the classroom environment. I had been referred by a friend to an interim superintendent who suggested I meet with Julie Clark, the teacher in their alternate education program (the special-needs students).

Mrs. Clark graciously accepted my offer and, within a couple of weeks, we embarked on a four-day project that fit beautifully into her "Career Investigations" class. The procedure was simple:

1. Each student would complete a six-minute ProScan survey—an exercise that would yield a twenty-page personal development report.
2. I would facilitate the curriculum in her one-hour class from Tuesday through Friday, working with her students on the subjects of self awareness and understanding, personal development, and a discussion of—and preparation for—the workforce, which was based on each student's assessment.

The students began their assignment by completing the short ProScan behavioral survey on a Friday morning in preparation for our Tuesday class. I will never forget walking into the classroom on that first Tuesday morning—April 17, 2001—because I thought I had the wrong room. The setting resembled a milder, more modern version of the 1970s TV sitcom, *Welcome Back, Kotter*. (For those too young to remember, the premise of that sitcom was wisecracking teacher Gabe Kotter returning to his high school alma mater to teach an often-unruly group of remedial loafers known as the "Sweat Hogs.") In my present scenario, there was one student sitting on the floor and another sitting on the window ledge, while another boy and girl had their arms wrapped around each other although they were sitting in different chairs. Others mingled as if they were on a social break. There was no order and, clearly, Mrs. Clark was unable to hold their attention.

As the mild-mannered teacher conducted my introduction, the students seemed to have little regard for a visiting guest. As I stood there, my first thought was what a mistake it was for me to be there. I may have overreacted as I raised my voice to explain that my donation of time and effort was to help them, but if they were going to be ungrateful and unreceptive, I would have to leave. It was during that moment that I explained the concept of professional courtesy—and told them that, in order to stay on schedule, I needed their cooperation.

Almost immediately, a student stood and headed for the door. I stepped in front of him and urged him to reconsider, promising to help him if he stayed. I stressed that I was not going to embarrass anyone and that the process would be interesting—maybe even fun. To my surprise, he returned to his seat and was attentive throughout the week.

After about fifteen minutes, the students' uneasiness subsided. For me, however, I was anxious while trying to disarm the potential for a mass exodus during the entire hour. The turning point came when I began to introduce the ProScan technology and how I applied personal process of introducing them to themselves. From that moment on, I had their full attention, and we began to connect. As I moved around the classroom, personally introducing each of the students to themselves and to their classmates, they clearly "got it" and appeared to enjoy the strangely entertaining visitor who knew them so well. The week flew by, and they grew exceptionally tolerant of me—almost kind. My only regret was that my time with them was so short.

Those fourteen students were good kids and I applaud teachers like Mrs. Clark who approach their students with persistence in the hope of making a difference. Each student had a story of hardship, and as we began to connect, the obstacles they had put between us began to unravel. Some were barely graduating from high school. As I learned of their different stories, they brought tears to my eyes, as it made me wonder how they were going to survive without falling victim to the system.

In particular, there was a senior named Gina, who lived in her grandmother's home with her boyfriend and their baby, her mother, and her mother's boyfriend—while working two jobs. Another student I remember was John, who was frightened to be homeless, was trying to find a job and, yet, had experienced the joy of buying his first car. That one hundred fifty-dollar set of wheels needed much work, but surely had the potential to take him places. (How well I remember that feeling.)

That week had a profound effect on my life as I observed a sample of how those teenagers existed within a system that simply did not understand them. I wondered if anyone other than Mrs. Clark even cared about what was going to happen to them.

How Does Someone with Special Needs Succeed?

- The students feel flawed.
- The parents understand that their children are a little slower or different from others, and wonder how to help them.
- The teachers have a difficult task, coping with challenging behaviors and trying to make it through another year.
- Other students create peer pressures that reinforce the students' impressions of being flawed, complete with destructive bullying and verbal comments.

What would it be like if parents and administrators could immediately understand the kids who need our help? What would it be like for the students if we could prevent them from falling into this category by having the ability to teach them, based on who they are and not by trying to fit them into "the system"? What would the educational system be like if we could eliminate the category of "special need" altogether?

Our week together proved that these young adults could be exceptional students. They were courteous and respectful, engaging, and—at least for our time together—they were not members of a "special needs" class. That week reinforced my desire to develop the "All Students Must Excel" program by taking our technology and training into the "personal" side of education.

As a testament to the success of the program, I received the following letter from Mrs. Clark:

> *Dear Mr. Crosby:*
>
> *My students found the ProScan personality assessments very informative. This information about themselves will be a benefit to them right now in their personal lives and in the future when they choose their careers. The majority of my students found this to be a relevant experience, and they began to see how to use their personality traits in a positive way instead of viewing them as faults or hindrances to success.*
>
> *If the students in class will apply the information you have equipped them with, they should be able to make career choices that they will continue to find enjoyable and challenging throughout their lives. Thank you once again for taking your time and for supplying them with a valuable tool for both their present lives and their futures.*
>
> *I have enclosed comments written by students in class about the presentation and the materials you have given them.*
>
> *Sincerely,*
>
> *Julie Clark*
> *Teacher of Alternate Education*

Mrs. Clark also included with her letter fourteen testimonials written by her students. Three of them follow:

Dear Mr. Crosby,

During our class with you, I learned that I have some good qualities and that I am important. When I am home, I do not think that highly of myself.

Gina

Dear Mr. Crosby,

I am writing to you to say thanks for your time for doing those ProScan sheets to help me know who I am, and learn about my stress which overall helped me learn more about myself.

Roger (the student who had started walking out at the beginning of the class)

Dear Mr. Crosby:

I am writing you this letter of appreciation to tell you how much I learned about myself in just the first day. Your survey is very close, if not right on. Just about everything you told me about myself was right. I can work good with people and get very controlling. Well, I just wanted to say thanks again and I am glad you came to our class. See Ya.

Sincerely,

Terry

From the Classroom to the School Board

While working with the Michigan Association of School Boards (MASB) on implementing PDP, as described in Chapter 7, Dr. Carl Hartman also was an unofficial liaison between superintendents and school boards, since he once filled the role as a school superintendent and because of his experience assisting school boards with their superintendent searches.

Intrigued by the PDP technology and the possibilities of helping school boards identify the right candidate choice, Dr. Hartman said to me, "There is someone here you need to meet," and we walked to the other side of the building to be introduced to Justin King, the executive director of MASB.

Eventually, MASB became a proficient client of our technology, leveraging the job-matching component in their many superintendent searches. Through his search activity, Dr. Hartman received phone calls from school board presidents and superintendents in need of assistance in facilitating their behavioral disagreements. Carl would quickly tell them they needed my help, and would refer them to me. From these referrals came the opportunity for me to work with dozens of schools in various communities in Michigan, thus enabling me to gain a wealth of knowledge in the new industry.

How Many Student Suicides Are Too Many?

One of my last projects before Carl Hartman and Justin King retired from MASB was a speaking engagement for the annual conference of the National Superintendent Search Association. During one of the breaks in the conference, a woman approached me with a very interesting question: "Was your program ever used to detect student suicidal tendencies?" When I asked why, she sadly explained that her husband was the superintendent of a school district that had experienced three suicides during the past year.

A few weeks later, Justin and I discussed the situation with that woman's husband and several other school officials. I agreed to facilitate a *pro bono* pilot program in the school district to determine its feasibility as an ongoing program. I was convinced that if I demonstrated the ability to understand and communicate with a small group of their most troubled students, we could actually start a program to assess student natural behaviors and stresses.

The school counselor selected eight students to participate, based upon the severity of their individual social and academic statuses. In seven out of eight of their homes, divorce and complicated parental relationships were significant factors. We invited both parents, along with their child, to participate, but in all cases, only the mothers attended. (Two fathers completed their assessments but did not take part in the telephone interview segment.)

My goal was to review the students' behavioral assessments without any history or consequences of their situations. During my calls, I also learned of their various physical attributes, including hair color, tattoos, and piercings. They all participated by validating the accuracy of their personal reports, and each student was respectful and conducted themselves unlike a troubled teen. The results were conclusive as I was able to connect quickly with each student. The ability and willingness of the students to trust in one sixty-minute conversation mystified their parents and counselor. I really expected this to be the beginning of an exciting pilot project.

However, after we were done, the counselor called and thanked me for my time and contributions to their program, but said she was too busy to lead any new projects.

All Students Must Excel[9]

After participating in one of my team sessions, the prominent superintendent of a large public school questioned me about my educational goal. To his surprise, my response took about ten seconds: "To change

---

9 All Students Must Excel© is a program from the Education Division of Global Behavior Companies, LLC.

the outcome of traditional education." His reaction was: "Wow, now that is an ambitious statement that sounds impressive, but it is probably unrealistic, don't you think?"

At that time, I said "no," and that is still my answer. We have to start somewhere, and I believe we begin by changing our attitudes at the top of education and by using the "New ABCs." We can make a fresh, positive impact on our children and, thus, naturally revive the entire field of education. Yes, the challenge is a massive process and possible.

When Justin King and Carl Hartman retired from the Michigan Association of School Boards, I contacted them to join Dr. Dan Wertz, a retired superintendent of schools, and me, so that we could create an educational dream team. Carl was a certified client administrator and Justin was a believer in my processes, because he had witnessed the results from his staff, executive board, and school executives. They had all known one another for years and represented the necessary talent to drive and administer the All Students Must Excel program—a program which I had created to address exorbitant student dropout rates and had wanted to release for years.

Mission/Goal of All Students Must Excel

The goal of the program is to increase the high school student graduation rate and improve the learning experience for students through teacher empowerment.

Currently in our schools, at-risk students are at an all-time high, resulting in violence, substance abuse, bullying, teen pregnancies, and suicides. All Students Must Excel will provide students and teachers with a knowledge and understanding of one another based upon each person's unique behavioral makeup, thus opening the channels of communication between student, parent, and teacher.

For many years, businesses have successfully used a science of measuring behavior technology developed by Professional DynaMetrics Program (PDP) to hire the most effective employees for open positions and to improve interactive relationships in the workplace.

All Students Must Excel will apply this same technology in the educational arena. The process of utilizing the PDP technology will eliminate the learning curve inherent in understanding each year's new group of students, overcoming misunderstandings, and improving how students, parents, and teachers work effectively with one another.

To be successful in working effectively with at-risk students, the All Students Must Excel program should run a minimum for two consecutive school years, assessing each participating student, parent, and teacher, twice a year. This program is designed for middle through high school grades.

Desired Outcomes of All Students Must Excel

- Increase student academic performance
- Decrease high student dropout rate
- Reduce bullying offenses, teen pregnancies, and suicides

How All Students Must Excel Will Work

- Students will learn to understand themselves and why they may feel misunderstood.
- Teachers, counselors, and social workers will be able to better identify potential "at-risk" students.
- Teachers will learn how to understand their students accurately and quickly.

- Teachers will learn to have effective, open, and direct dialog with students.

What All Students Must Excel Will Address

- The correlation of behaviors among at-risk students, ADD, and ADHD
- The need for discipline and conflict resolution
- The need for learning plans based upon a combination of students' learning styles and educators' teaching styles
- The overall behavioral patterns of each individual school, its students, teachers, and parents
- Student stress and morale issues
- Student energy and energy drains
- Teacher energy and energy drains
- Teacher morale and job satisfaction
- Bullying
- Teacher retention

Why All Students Must Excel Has Stalled

In an area as important as education where emotional pain runs high for students, parents, teachers, and school administrators, it is hard to understand how a program such as this could fail to launch. Even so, recently, several school executives who initially approved the program failed to follow through.

In Denver, Colorado, Joe Dowd, a long-time PDP friend and colleague (who is actually the first and most accomplished licensee to work with PDP founder Bruce M. Hubby), successfully helped organizations in many vertical markets and has a great story in education. He kindly offered his support and permission to contact one of his clients to personally discuss how Aims Community College applied PDP with their administration and the school witnessed how well it worked with their staff and students. Joe trained the staff at Aims and helped them utilize their PDPWorks system to teach at-risk students through the alternative high school diploma program operated through Aims Community College. The result? Their graduation rate went from 54 percent to 90 percent.

Carl, Justin and I discussed the issues of high dropout and poor grade point averages with a select group of influential educators from a public school in central Michigan. This was our second meeting and joining our conference call was Marsha Harmon, the training coordinator for Aims College, who had a chance to share her story of how using the PDP technology succeeded at their school in Greely, Colorado.

There we were—my elite group—passionately communicating how understanding their students could deliver an unprecedented return on investment to the students, the school district, and the community. However, the concept of knowing a student so well seemed almost too good to be true. Although the school had extreme problems and the dropout rate was unacceptable, the educators failed to believe that All Students Must Excel was a possible solution to help the students, parents, and teachers.

Instead of moving forward with the program, they simply became "too busy" to consider the project. Not one of these paid-to-make-a-difference educators followed through to complete the six-minute ProScan survey as they previously agreed prior to our meetings. They hired a new superintendent shortly thereafter and, although we felt we had made a positive impression on them, they failed to introduce the possibilities of a solution to the new administration.

Each school we spoke to had its own story of change and indecision, and each time we presented our program, another set of extreme conditions and obstacles emerged and dictated the repeated outcome of non-committal. What we have learned by attempting to engage in business with schools is how to understand the behaviors which are common among large populations of educators. For instance: each educator has a similar story. As they move from high school to higher learning and into teaching, most of them only know the educational system—not the world of business, or any other outside study. Some desire more than teaching, and those few venture into leadership roles in hopes of becoming a superintendent.

Most superintendents find themselves as influential educators who have fallen into the political drama of the school board, the teachers' union, and the parents—all under the spotlight of the media. They are smart, passionate people who have been stopped at the crossroads between education and policy. Of the superintendents we met, we found that their ability to be entrepreneurial was almost non-existent. The opportunity to launch All Students Must Excel has stalled for many of the same reasons: the challenges behind the phenomenon of behavior.

There are those who have the leadership behavior sufficient to try something different and to take something which has been proven in the business community and move it into the school and family. Assuring other educators—who are more cautious and prefer to maintain the status quo until retirement—that they have the authority to instigate change is a bit more challenging. "Bill Gates has called America's high schools 'obsolete,' while Oprah Winfrey has said that our nation is in a 'state of emergency' because of them. Former U.S. Secretary of Education Rod Paige has called them an 'unrecognized educational crisis.'" [10]

---

10 Jason Amos, "Dropouts, Diplomas and Dollars, U.S. High Schools and the Nation's Economy," *Alliance for Excellent Education*, Washington, DC, 2008,

The purpose of the All Students Must Excel program is "to change the outcome of traditional education." From the perspective of an educator, this concept may be too aggressive, but from the viewpoint of a dreamer and entrepreneurial businessperson, all things are possible. The stereotypical educator cannot cure our problems in education. Only those who know no boundaries can cure them.

Chapter Nugget

Since the early days of education, students have simply aspired to learn and to be understood. By understanding the natural behaviors of students, parents, and teachers, clear lines of communication can be drawn and tensions can be reduced. The ProScan assessment tool can also provide the playbook that empowers teachers to educate students—from the silent ones to those of the high-energy variety. Eliminating the learning curve when teachers and students meet is a priceless tool for understanding every student during the first week of school rather than using the entire year to summarize individual potentials.

"One of the unfortunate things about our education system is that we do not teach students how to avail themselves of their subconscious capabilities."
-- Bill Lear

---

accessed June 30, 2014, http://www.all4ed.org.

CHAPTER 9

CHURCHES AND HUMAN BEHAVIOR

"It is not by the gray of the hair that one knows the age of the heart."
-- Edward Bulwer-Lytton

This chapter validates the importance to understand The Why You Do to enhance all of your experiences and relationships and does not exclude those at your place of worship.

Natural Human Behavior Seeks Spiritual Direction

Monasteries and churches are places where people typically have sought the solace of holy men and women for forgiveness, direction, and spiritual wisdom. Our society and the times in which we live are complicated with distractions, torments, and pressures of uncertainty. Today, when church members face pressures within their marriages or their family lives, they still turn to their most trusted resource—their church leadership.

The church is a melting pot of people seeking refuge from life's challenges, while looking for breakthroughs to resolve their problems. Quite simply, most of our church organizations cannot handle this level of demand. By comparison, the need is equivalent to having an outpatient medical service in a community that really needs a full-service hospital. Parents are hungry for the "right answers" for their families, the workplace is tentative, and schools must perform miracles with children from broken homes and shattered lives.

God created human beings for spiritual relationships. Therefore, we have a natural instinct to crave spiritual belonging. Unfortunately, the behavioral problems that people have in their daily lives often spill over into their church lives.

Human Behavior within the Church

You have probably heard that we will never find the perfect church as long as *people* attend. As pointed out in Chapter 1, we all have our early personal and family stories, and some of our most memorable experiences have taken place in church. Whether positive or negative, these experiences leave a lasting impression on a person's future belief structure.

A few months ago, I had the chance to discuss the subject of memorable church experiences over a cup of coffee with my close friend, Cody. We talked about our childhood church memories, and he enthusiastically asked me about my own recollections. As I began to describe the concept that "we all have a story," his face lit up and he related a story about his mother:

One summer, during his early childhood, he and his family witnessed their mother suffering from a serious skin allergy. She patiently dealt with the torment, as finding comfort during the long, hot summer was difficult without the luxury of central air conditioning. Cody and his family had recently relocated, and, upon finding a new church home, each Sunday the family would get dressed up to meet new people in their small congregation. As church attendance became their weekly regimen, a core group of women appeared troubled by his mother's appearance, because she always wore slacks, rather than a more church-appropriate dress or skirt. Eventually, she realized their consternation over her attire. Cody explained, "When Mom found out, we stopped going to church because her feelings were hurt! But the sad part was that this social rejection only increased her anxiety." What these judgmental women did not know was that her legs was severely scarred by the skin allergy, and she felt she had to keep them covered at all times.

A church is not unlike any other social environment where personal offenses occur. However, in a church setting, we expect our spiritual family to have more tolerance than those people we encounter in the office or home. We expect less judgment, but more grace and acceptance, allowing us to be authentic.

Some people attend church out of a natural void that only a spiritual relationship can fill. Traditionally, parents feel one of their first obligations in raising a family is to cultivate and nurture a firm foundation of values and belief structures. Over the years, I have heard a number of speakers proclaim, "We raise chickens, ducks and cows. When our children are the subject, we have a greater duty than just raising them. We must teach, lead, and develop them for life's great challenges." Cody journeyed through life experiencing alcoholism and making poor choices, but he did not have a hardened heart toward the church. He has a sad memory of his mother's pain and its affect on his family, but today, he is an accomplished Bible teacher and facilitator in my men's prayer ministry and church prison ministry.

I know of a man who died an atheist because of the pressure and influence of his parents. With an angry tone, he once told me, "They were hypocrites! They preached one perspective, but did not live the lifestyle." They tried so hard to make him serve a religion that they pushed him away from a personal relationship with God. He lived his entire adult life struggling to accept the biblical principle of God's creation. He died with a heart full of unrest and rebellion.

Ministry after Breakfast

Some of the most valuable conversations I have had in getting to know others came through sharing brunch with new acquaintances—particularly couples—after a Sunday church service. Over the years, my wife, Kathleen, and I have done this quite frequently. Somewhere interwoven into the discussion, the question always arose, "Don, exactly *what* do you do?" My response to this question is often simply this: "I am a Behavioral Locksmith. I help people unlock their behavioral challenges in the home and workplace using a state-of-the-art behavioral assessment tool called ProScan." After hearing this, the conversation has often taken off like a red traffic light that has just tuned green. The mood changes and moves from the status quo to how many years of unhappiness they have had as a couple, or how their children have struggled with others or how their teachers do not understand them.

More Real Family Issues

When Matthew was ten years old, his parents—dear friends of mine—were perplexed by their son's behavior. They did not understand why he was so tired that he did not have the desire to play football. He was smart, yet he struggled with his grades. After finishing one of Kathleen's extraordinary meals following a Sunday church service, Matthew's parents opened up to us and asked if I could shed some light on Matthew's challenges. Other than the assessments performed on my two nephews, nine-year-old Tyler, and seven-year-old Jacob, I had not used the assessments on other children, and I wondered if a ProScan survey could accurately measure Matthew's young, struggling behavior.

Within a few minutes, Matthew completed the ProScan process as intelligently as many adults could. As I moved through the results with Matt and his parents, they confirmed the results to be "spot on."

Matthew is a great kid—one of my favorites. He was energetic, trouble-prone, and mischievous, but well meaning. Together with his high energy and extreme passion, he was very misunderstood by adults, but fearless around his peers. With this mix, no dare would go untaken, and he would often act before thinking. He was a terrific young person who wanted to do things without drama, and did not want to be in trouble, yet he could not understand why he could be so disobedient.

By having his ProScan assessment, Matthew's parents were able to exercise every option to help him through challenging moments, talking him through the emotional rollercoaster of behavioral calamities, using strict discipline and tough love effectively. Even at a young age Matthew was able to understand and accept why he was making these bad decisions and he worked hard to adjust his behavior all through school. When Matthew graduated from high school, he left for Chicago to join the United States Navy. He has matured through his adolescent behavior to become a responsible adult who has a plan.

Even Pastors Can Have Marital Problems

Just last week, Kathleen and I were catching up with close friends and learned that one of the pastors of our former church has recently divorced and remarried. The pastor and his wife had been sweethearts from their first meeting at a youth camp. During college, their attraction grew, and they went through the usual rigors of pre-marriage counseling. They soon married and were the ideal couple. They had a family and, after twenty-four years, called their relationship quits. Sadly, this has occurred too many times to too many wonderful church leaders. Couples who have been dedicated to the ministry for so many years serving others often cannot make their own marriages last, and, as a result, they drift apart.

In 1994, we leased a townhome in Woodland Hills, California, as we were expanding our business from Hawaii to the mainland. Shortly after our arrival, a close friend introduced us to an awesome church in the Simi Valley and its pastor. Very soon, we built a relationship with the pastor and his family, who impressed us by their dedication and spiritual life. They seemed to be living well in a picture-perfect setting.

I will never forget being invited to their home for dinner to introduce the ProScan assessment and conduct a modest comparison of the pastor and his wife's reports. The pastor was in the planning stage of scheduling a marriage retreat for the congregation and considered adding our tool and my participation during a weekend getaway. After the pastor's wife completed her assessment, I began to scroll through the graphs, mentally comparing their extreme differences and silently pondering their potential conflicts. I kept telling myself that they would be fine. They were, after all, smart people, who seemed to love one another and their three accomplished children. They knew the Bible, feared God, and walked in the Scriptures through memory verse teaching, even at the dinner table.

The marriage retreat seemed successful by the large turnout and shared comments, but sadly, their marriage did not survive. They separated and divorced sometime during the following year. Regardless of the information they obtained from comparing their assessments, they choose not to work out their differences and their marriage failed.

It seems so easy for good people to become tired of one another's temperaments and give up on their relationships.

Why Some Volunteers Stop Volunteering

There are many reasons why people stop volunteering, but generally it is centered around offenses caused by miscommunication, which is predictable if you understand everyone's behavior. So the value of having a ProScan behavioral assessment on everyone volunteering is critical to reducing the miscommunications. While casually talking with a group of my closest friends, I broached the subject of why volunteers sometimes cease to be a volunteer. Two words summed up my friends' responses: burnout and offense. One of them described a situation where he and his wife had passionately volunteered in their church, and after a few months of involvement, their positions suddenly changed. They tried to adjust to the new protocol and style of their new leader, but it just did not work. They remained for as long as they could, but eventually departed from the volunteer corps because the leadership failed to assign the right person in the right position. They became offended and eventually left the church they had once loved.

A person's communication style is often the culprit that causes offenses. We are supposed to gather for kingdom reasons, and yet, too often we separate because of behavioral disconnection. Generally, it is a "heart condition" combined with a behavioral condition. Recognizing our natural styles is so important that slowing down from the real pressures of life and checking one's heart is critical to improving our relationships as we serve. The inclusive value of the nonprofit organization is built on the strength of the volunteer staff. As with employees, not only must volunteers possess the gifts and skills to perform tasks, but they also need the ability to follow through with "servanthood," grace, and forgiveness.

In order to prevent negative repercussions, volunteers need to be given clear instructions and a process to pursue excellence. Exceptional leadership will observe certain behaviors within their volunteer staff and pair the people with those behaviors with the essential functions of what needs to be accomplished. Volunteers should receive well deserved appreciation based on their contribution. They need to be understood and given clear instruction so they can succeed in their involvement in any project.

Occasionally, along with the virtuous intentions of donating our time, something changes. The expectations of the commitment become different, or there is a misunderstood feature about how much time is actually required (e.g., previously undisclosed follow-up phone calls, emails, committees, and meetings) than originally expected. Situations change and get mixed up very easily. Another pitfall is, periodically, as weeks turn into months, we find ourselves "owning" a position. When that happens, the emotional obligation overrides the initial purpose of giving of one's time and the cause becomes one's personal ministry, with all sorts of ownership issues in the mix.

Perhaps volunteer positions should come with an expiration date and a renewal clause. The important thing is to have the ability to pinpoint each volunteer's behavior quickly and accurately. It is wise to try to eliminate the frustration and disappointment that can possibly develop with volunteering. The church has a serious responsibility to be biblically accountable, and yet to draw people close as a safe haven from the battles of the outside world. The willingness and disposition to serve others is the essence of loving others above our personal needs.

Church Administration, Hiring, Firing, and Managing Leadership

Church leaders have comparable challenges to those who manage "for profit" businesses. Common within church environments is the sensitive nature of people working and having fellowship together. Administering and hiring through the human equation of a church organization is probably the most difficult and stressful responsibility of the position. The mix of personal sensitivity, emotion, and financial issues brings leaders to their knees seeking spiritual guidance and knowledge. Selecting the right people is naturally difficult. The question for those in power needs to be: "What is the most effective and appropriate process for hiring and managing the workforce for the church?"

Generally, the process of how church administrators implement their hiring decisions is with intuition, instinct, and feeling. The new employees, then, become the responsibility of someone else to manage. This common process actually creates the most complicated results. When the trigger is pulled and the decision is made, the hiring decision is over—but the relationship has just begun.

The *most* common—and least complicated—decision is simply to continue using your present traditional, intuitive implementation to hire and manage by perception and natural instinct.

We have all known wonderful men and woman of God who have struggled with the "people" component of running their organizations, including:

- Hiring, managing, communicating, and leading staff.
- Counseling missionaries stressed with their own marital and family issues.
- Understanding, motivating, and empowering volunteers. (The concept is simple, yet profound. Throughout the Bible, there is a noble emphasis on achieving understanding and wisdom.)

Consider using the power of science to help with church administration, people, staffing, counseling, and helping missionaries. The body of Christ can be empowered with the use of science to improve relationships and to replace conflicts and disappointments with knowledge. Because people will continue to misunderstand other people, we should emotionally try to prepare ourselves for "the next time." I am not suggesting we go looking for drama, but we must realize that, when we least expect conflict, drama can find us anywhere—even when we are seeking spiritual fellowship.

The only way I know how to approach this unpleasant difficulty is to eliminate the painful experience with forgiveness, shake it off emotionally by reminding myself not to accept things personally, and to care for the others involved—and even to love them unconditionally. We can disagree with their issues or behaviors, but it is not acceptable to fall into the trap of disconnection. As soon as we start to dislike a person, it creates the offense—the walls come up and it is the end. We must be cautious not to permit our behavioral reactions, emotions, or issues—or those of anyone else—to separate us from our friends, family, church, or personal relationship with Almighty God.

Chapter Nugget

As long as people focus their faith on idols rather than on God, disappointment will always ensue. Don't expect too much from attending church because pastors and their leaders are not there to "fix" you. Among other things, they are there to teach and encourage through the Word of God. Attending church is meant for worshipping in community and creating Godly relationships.

"The Greatest Commandment—You shall love the Lord your God with all your heart, with all your soul, and with all your mind. This is the first and greatest commandment. And the second is like it: 'You shall love your neighbor as yourself.'"

-- Matthew 22:37-39, NIV

SECTION THREE
A TOOL TO MEASURE BEHAVIOR

Chapters 10-12 moves from navigating the circumstances of life to measuring behavior with a statistical tool, the outcomes of which are endless.

CHAPTER 10

EVEN THE FIRST WHEEL WAS CREATED WITH TOOLS

"There is no instrument so deceptive as the mind."
-- St. John Ervine

Proper Tools Provide Better Results

The process of completing a task becomes more natural when combining the right tool with the proper instruction. In every profession, there are instruments, appliances, or machinery necessary for producing the final product or service. The quality of the tool affects the outcome. In the kitchen, it is the stove, the cookware, or the knives. In the office, it is the computer, software, printer, and scanner. In manufacturing, a variety of machinery and devices at different cell group stations contributes to the final product. In farming, there are tractors, plows, planters, choppers, and combines. Golfers have particular clubs, favorite drivers, and dozens of different balls. Not every tool is the same; each has its own utility and unique design. With automation and ingenuity, inventions give us today's exquisite luxuries.

Behavioral Misunderstandings

For the moment, let's consider the philosophy that behavioral misunderstandings evolved from biblical times, and the possibility that the most reliable application to untangle such a theory would be the use of statistics. So to explore this theory, let's create a hypothetical journey that mankind has been searching for generations upon generations to find the validation research and, when we do, we finally discover the scientific antidote in the form of a behavioral tool.

Personality Tools

Generally, the manner in which a person responds to the challenge of learning about him- or herself with either acceptance or skepticism is driven by that person's natural behaviors and experiences. There are vast collections of interesting tests, assessments, and survey tools that provide information on recognizing personality traits, most of which are not particularly understood by the average consumer. Recently, I even heard a nationally syndicated radio advertisement for car insurance, describing many insurance companies as just another "personality test." How do you find the most appropriate technology for your needs?

Considering that not all personality and behavioral technologies are created equally, they do not have to be complicated, expensive, or difficult to administer—while still complying with state and federal government regulations.

The Law of Difference

Just because two ideas are similar when viewed from the outside, putting them in the same category does not make them equal. Not all cars are the same, although they all have four wheels and drive down the road; and while soft drinks are packaged in similar bottling they, too, have particular variances. Thousands of products fall into similar categories, but all have distinct differences. After all, having a pizza at one restaurant does not mean having a pizza everywhere is going to taste the same. When considering a new behavioral technology, remember that each program has its own unique qualities.

When people ask me what I do, and as I begin to introduce how I help people with the ProScan tool, many roll their eyes and look at me with a facial expression which says "oh no, not another one!" When this reaction emerges, the only evidence that will readjust anyone's opinion is to have them personally experience the process, ease, and depth of what the tool measures.

A few weeks ago, while I was working on a project in Mexico, my expert interpreter, methodically—and almost poetically—described his ProScan experience. He said that, having been groomed by his mother as a young man and experiencing the complexity of languages, he had mentally and emotionally struggled with how a person could effectively learn a new language from a "How To" program, until he experienced the "Rosetta Stone" program. He described how transforming the experience was when he realized (and accepted) how good their learning system works.

He went on to say: "Don, this week I have experienced the similar thought-provoking clarity of witnessing all of these people (about thirty Mexican workers) begin to really understand themselves through the ProScan report and your introduction. As the interpreter, I am amazed with their confirmation, the accuracy, and their reception. This is so different than anything I've ever seen or been exposed to."

The difference between PDP and other assessment inventories is what it measures, and the mathematics of how it measures human behavior with such depth and precision.

You Are Here!

As a sixteen-year-old boy, one of my most memorable road trip adventures was with two seventeen-year-old close friends from high school en route from St. Johns, Michigan, to Ft. Lauderdale, Florida, for spring break. The three of us literally stuffed ourselves into my barely heated 1961 VW Bug and wrapped ourselves in sleeping bags to prevent frostbite.

The journey had actually begun a year earlier than that cold morning when we pulled out of my driveway bound for teenage glory. My father had purposely bought the VW because it needed work. He took me to Clinton National Bank, where I borrowed one hundred dollars to accompany my seventy-five-dollar down payment—my very first auto loan. The engine ran well, the heater blew air barely warmer than my own breath, and its body was a rust bucket—a cream-colored, ugly set of wheels that no fifteen-year-old would want to be seen driving. It was very different from my desired Ford Mustang or Chevy Nova. As I placed my hand through the floorboard and tried to get my dad to realize that the car was not such a good deal, he continued to press on. "Besides," he said, "it is too late. You own it!" He had made the decision for me, and somehow, I had to make it work.

In my opinion, the car was certified junk, so I needed professional help. Who better to talk to than the people who fixed cars for a living? So I visited a body shop to observe and learn how the process worked. After a few days, I caught the vision of my new car's potential, but I knew it was going to take a lot of time, money, and work. Finally, the picture was clear in my mind. This was not a big deal—I pictured myself driving to California with my tricked-out Bug, pulling up to California show cars on the Sunset Strip. The potential of what the car would become fired my ambition to complete the restoration.

Understand that this was *not*, by far, a father-and-son project; it was more of an exam—a life lesson for me to prove myself. It took countless late nights in the tool shed at the mercy of the ever-changing, seasonal Michigan weather, with limited heat and floodlights. That car had so much "Bondo" plastic filler that I was afraid it would fly off in sheets when we were passed on the road by a sixteen-wheeler semi truck.

But, once I was done, we were ready to go on spring break. Painted "candy apple blue," with wide chrome wheels on oversized red-wall tires, the car looked like it belonged on the beach. I will never forget the difficulty I had selling that road trip to my parents, as they said I was too young. I believe their final approval came as they discussed my dedication and accomplishment of fixing up that car—the trip was my reward for completing my life lesson.

From left to right: Dick Holm, Don Chant, and the author, from the author's family album.

Real life is similar to that road trip. My desire was to go faster, but that loaded-down Bug could hardly get out of its own way, and it felt at times as if we were actually going to roll backwards while driving through the mountains. It seemed that we drove for years to get to Florida, while our music played repeatedly. My sound system was an eight-track tape deck, and we had a modest collection of the latest hits of the Rolling Stones and Beatles, which carried us through the trip. I will never forget how we looked forward to studying the large wall map at each rest area to see how far we had *rolled*. At each stop, the road map boldly announced, "YOU ARE HERE," which was printed inside a star. Seeing where we were in proximity to our final destination gave us clarity—and the eventual realization that we were actually going to make it.

In life—just as on that trip—unless we can actually see where we are and who we are, we will aimlessly drive around without knowing how to adjust to the conditions necessary to arrive at our final destination.

Graphic by Timmy Cai.

Your Personal Roadmap

We had a great Florida trip on that spring break but, honestly, I do not think the VW Bug could have sustained finding our way to California. We completed a successful journey because we had followed our plan and the directions. Compared to using a road map for going in the right way, planning your future requires an understanding of your natural self to assist in the prevention of becoming lost to reactions and unfortunate circumstances. How will you predict the outcome of important decision making without understanding yourself accurately?

Here is a sample ProScan Intensity Chart of the basic/natural self–the way you would function if there were no outside pressures for adjustment. On this one page, you will travel from trait to trait to see a "snapshot" description of measuring personal individuality. The location of the circles is the exact position of each particular trait and the shaded areas included in each column are other descriptors of less intensity.

ProScan Intensity Chart

Dominance Take Charge Trait	Extroversion People Trait	Pace Patience Trait	Conformity Systems Trait
Intimidating	Overwhelming	Resist change	Judgmental
Bold	Flamboyant	Unhurried	Perfectionistic
Forceful	Verbose	Determined	Uncompromising
Abrasive	Promoter	Tenacious	Exacting
Commanding	Convincing	Deliberate	Meticulous
Fearless	Gregarious	Persistent	Vigilant
Daring	Pleaser	Avoid conflict	Strict
Demanding	Effusive	Resilient	Orthodox
Authoritative	Eager	Sympathetic	Systematic
Courageous	Inspirational	Sensitive	Precise
Direct	Expressive	Warm	Prudent
Visionary	Empathetic	Harmonious	Diligent
Inventive	Trusting	Enduring	Conscientious
Venturous	Exciting	Steady	Dedicated
Quick-witted	Inclusive	Consistent	Disciplined
Analytical	Motivating	Thorough	Conventional
Firm	Articulate	Constant	Specialist
Competitive	Optimistic	Dependable	Procedural
Decisive	Sociable	Rhythmic	Focused
Definite	Responsive	Methodical	Dutiful
Assertive	Fun-loving	Informal	Loyal
Self-assured	Enthusiastic	Casual	Committed
Innovative	Persuasive	Good-natured	Detailed
Originator	Verbal	Cooperative	Accurate
Certain	Participative	Easy-going	Structured
Confident	Poised	Amiable	Careful
Curious	Friendly	Pleasant	Orderly
DynaMetric Mid-Line — Flexible / Adaptable	Flexible / Adaptable	Flexible / Adaptable	Flexible / Adaptable
Moderate	Sincere	Adjustability	Open-minded
Supportive	Congenial	Like change	Generalist
Amenable	Genuine	Versatile	Less-detailed
Collaborative	Composed	Active	Big-picture
Agreeable	Contemplative	Spirited	Independent
Modest	Considerate	Restless	Avoid detail
Accepting	Observant	Impatient	Free-spirited
Attentive	Imaginative	Mobile	Flexible
Helpful	Private	Dynamic	Creative
Discreet	Selective	Seek change	Unconventional
Tolerant	communicator	Lively	Individualistic
Non-competitive	Self-protective	Swift	Adventurous
Cautious	Mild-mannered	Driving	Free-thinker
Peaceable	Respectful	Pressing	Unconstrained
Gracious	Thinker	Hasty	Challenge rules
Accommodating	Reflective	Spontaneous	Carefree
Gentle	Unpretentious	Instantaneous	Autonomous
Humble	Quiet	Fast-paced	Uninhibited
Temperate	Introspective	Impulsive	Self-governing
Undemanding	Reserved	Impetuous	Non-detailed
Deferring	Shy	Impelling	Free-wheeling
Non-controlling	Circumspect	Abrupt	Resistant
Tentative	Skeptical	Coiled-spring	Controversial
Hesitant	Confidential	Sporadic	Contrary
Placid	Guarded	Short-fused	Anti-bureaucratic
Yielding	Undemonstrative	Volatile	Adversarial
Complacent	Solitary	Explosive	Nonconforming
Supportive	**Reserved**	**Urgent**	**Independent**

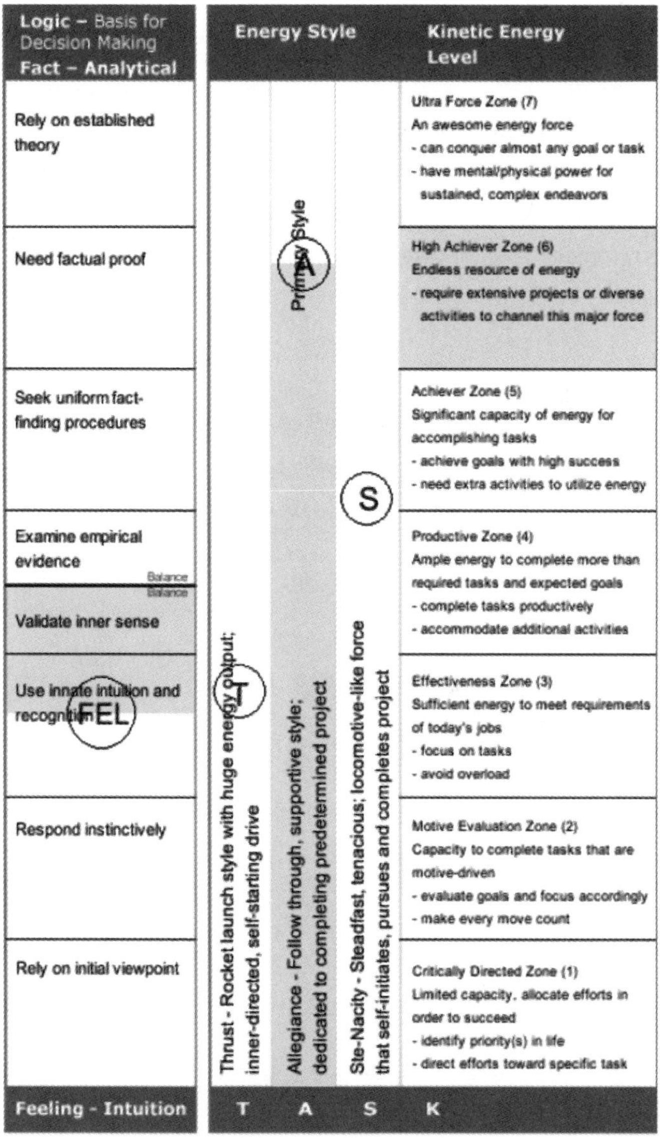

Logic – Basis for Decision Making Fact – Analytical	Kinetic Energy Level
Rely on established theory	**Ultra Force Zone (7)** An awesome energy force - can conquer almost any goal or task - have mental/physical power for sustained, complex endeavors
Need factual proof	**High Achiever Zone (6)** Endless resource of energy - require extensive projects or diverse activities to channel this major force
Seek uniform fact-finding procedures	**Achiever Zone (5)** Significant capacity of energy for accomplishing tasks - achieve goals with high success - need extra activities to utilize energy
Examine empirical evidence Balance Balance Validate inner sense	**Productive Zone (4)** Ample energy to complete more than required tasks and expected goals - complete tasks productively - accommodate additional activities
Use innate intuition and recognition FEL	**Effectiveness Zone (3)** Sufficient energy to meet requirements of today's jobs - focus on tasks - avoid overload
Respond instinctively	**Motive Evaluation Zone (2)** Capacity to complete tasks that are motive-driven - evaluate goals and focus accordingly - make every move count
Rely on initial viewpoint	**Critically Directed Zone (1)** Limited capacity, allocate efforts in order to succeed - identify priority(s) in life - direct efforts toward specific task
Feeling - Intuition	T A S K

Energy Style

Primary Style

A S T

Thrust - Rocket launch style with huge energy output; inner-directed, self-starting drive

Allegiance - Follow through, supportive style; dedicated to completing predetermined project

Ste-Nacity - Steadfast, tenacious; locomotive-like force that self-initiates, pursues and completes project

The next chapter will further acquaint you with the ProScan technology, and the introduction from the inventor.

Chapter Nugget

Pursue excellence with an open mind and seek to gain understanding of your actual behavior so you know your true potential. Remember that the Swiss Army knife gained worldwide renown because it presented so many useful options, not only because it was an exceptional knife.

"If you wish to understand others you must intensify your own individualism."
-- Oscar Wilde

CHAPTER 11

MEASURING BEHAVIOR WITH THE PROSCAN TOOL

"A man should look for what is, and not for what he thinks should be."
-- Albert Einstein

Our Foundation

A foundation is "the lowest and supporting layer of a structure."[11] When the construction is complete, the foundation, although unseen, plays the most critical role in any building.

An exceptional personal foundation provides strength, safety, and longevity, as well as public and financial success. We each have a foundational core behavior known as the "Cornerstone Traits," hidden below the surface—a sort of behavioral DNA foundation that enables us to withstand the conditions of our life experiences.

---

11 "Foundation," *Wikipedia*, accessed June 30, 2014, http://en.wikipedia.org/wiki/Foundation.

PDP's foundation is based on these traits and using them in trait pairs will give an accurate predictability of an individual.

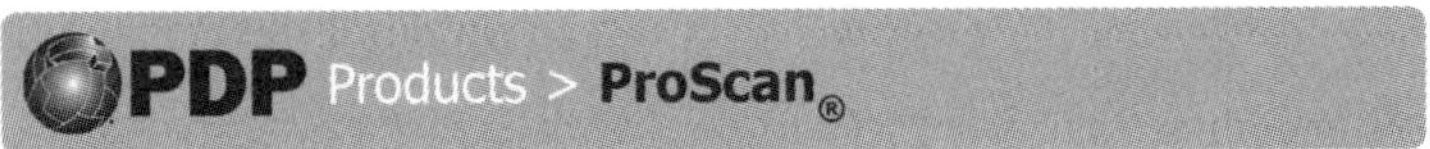

Four Cornerstone Behavioral Traits

DOMINANCE	EXTROVERSION	PACE	CONFORMITY
Take Charge Trait Act on the environment Control-oriented through things	Social/Relational Trait Act on the environment Control-oriented through people	Patience/Rate of Motion Trait Influenced by the environment Control-oriented through process	Systems Oriented/Quality Assurance Trait Conscious of the environment Control-oriented through rules
High Dominance Direct Decisive Innovative Competitive Get results Exert or challenge authority	High Extroversion Articulate Enthusiastic Interactive Persuasive and influential Seek opportunity Build teams Delegate technical tasks	High Pace Steady Consistent Persistent Dependable Cautious about change	High Conformity Structured Accurate Loyal Follow and maintain established systems and procedures perceived to be right
Flexible/ Adaptable	Flexible/ Adaptable	Flexible/ Adaptable	Flexible/ Adaptable DynaMetric Mid-Line
Low Dominance Supportive Moderate Collaborative	Low Extroversion Contemplative Private Imaginative	Low Pace Spontaneous Versatile Action-oriented with sense of urgency	Low Conformity Independent Value personal freedom and minimal external controls

WEB www.PDPglobal.com • APP www.PDPworks.com

The Introduction of ProScan

These days, people expect instant results, but there was a time when people criticized PDP for the speed-of-light assessment ability—especially when they compared our six-minute ProScan tool to other technologies whose completion time extended from thirty minutes to one and one-half hours. Now, because of other famous discoveries, ProScan's scientific process is more respected in the marketplace. The sheer brilliance of a quick and easy, yet highly accurate, behavioral measurement tool that simply measures more of human behavior is ahead of the pack. At a glance, this brief, self-scoring questionnaire seems unimpressive. But do not let its simplicity dissuade you from its ability to measure the complexity of human behavior.

The sixty adjectives contained in the questionnaire are mathematically "cross-matrixed" to one hundred forty-eight thousand behavioral factors for the on-line computer-processing program to produce uncompromisingly accurate descriptions.

Measuring More

Besides the "Cornerstone Traits," PDP also measures the traits of Logic (how a person makes decisions), Energy Styles (how a person accomplishes their goals and aspirations), and Kinetic Energy (how much energy a person has to sustain). All of this makes PDP robust and unique from other personality tools. (These traits are shown on the Trait Intensity Chart in Chapter 10.)

Profound with Ease

When you first compare the PDP reporting with other assessments, you will notice a few basic similarities of measurement, but don't let that stop you from going forward to experience the differences.

Without venturing too deeply into the technical "braininess" of how PDP determines the results, here are the behaviors quantified.

The complete behavior "is measured as PDP researchers have determined that every human being has three distinct aspects, or selves, which they refer to as profiles."[12]

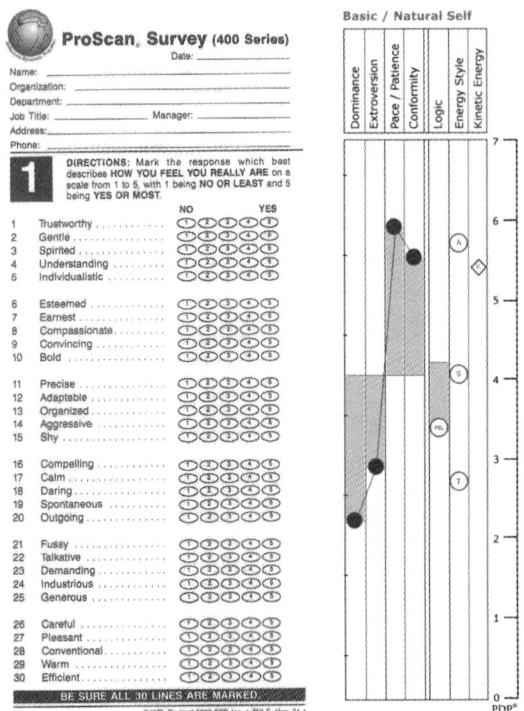

ProScan® Survey (400 Series)

Date: ______

Name: ______
Organization: ______
Department: ______
Job Title: ______ Manager: ______
Address: ______
Phone: ______

1 **DIRECTIONS:** Mark the response which best describes **HOW YOU FEEL YOU REALLY ARE** on a scale from 1 to 5, with 1 being **NO OR LEAST** and 5 being **YES OR MOST**.

		NO				YES
1	Trustworthy	1	2	3	4	5
2	Gentle	1	2	3	4	5
3	Spirited	1	2	3	4	5
4	Understanding	1	2	3	4	5
5	Individualistic	1	2	3	4	5
6	Esteemed	1	2	3	4	5
7	Earnest	1	2	3	4	5
8	Compassionate	1	2	3	4	5
9	Convincing	1	2	3	4	5
10	Bold	1	2	3	4	5
11	Precise	1	2	3	4	5
12	Adaptable	1	2	3	4	5
13	Organized	1	2	3	4	5
14	Aggressive	1	2	3	4	5
15	Shy	1	2	3	4	5
16	Compelling	1	2	3	4	5
17	Calm	1	2	3	4	5
18	Daring	1	2	3	4	5
19	Spontaneous	1	2	3	4	5
20	Outgoing	1	2	3	4	5
21	Fussy	1	2	3	4	5
22	Talkative	1	2	3	4	5
23	Demanding	1	2	3	4	5
24	Industrious	1	2	3	4	5
25	Generous	1	2	3	4	5
26	Careful	1	2	3	4	5
27	Pleasant	1	2	3	4	5
28	Conventional	1	2	3	4	5
29	Warm	1	2	3	4	5
30	Efficient	1	2	3	4	5

BE SURE ALL 30 LINES ARE MARKED.

©1979, Revised 2000 PDP, Inc. • 750 E. Hwy. 24 •

Side one of the ProScan Survey.

12 *A Living Legacy: The Man, the Research, the System*, 2nd ed (Colorado Springs, CO: PDP, Inc., 2013). Used with permission, by Brent W. Hubby, p.41.

As you can see, the directions are informal. A person simply marks the response which best describes HOW YOU FEEL YOU REALLY ARE on a scale from 1 to 5, with 1 being NO OR LEAST, and 5 being YES OR MOST.

The first thirty adjectives measure the Basic/Natural Self environment, which is how a person functions without any outside interferences. This is the most efficient and successful area to operate in, which reduces unwanted stresses. Within the Basic/Natural Self, here are the traits measured:

- The cornerstone traits (Dominance, Extroversion, Pace, and Conformity)
- How a person accomplishes goals and aspirations, Thrust, Allegiance, or "Stenacity" (a word which was coined to mean "being steadfast")
- How the candidate makes a decision: by fact, feeling, or balance of fact and feeling
- The person's Kinetic Energy—the potential energy a person has to invest into life. (PDP does a remarkable job of distinguishing the measurement of potential energy and the energy drain of how much a person has used with their life experiences.)

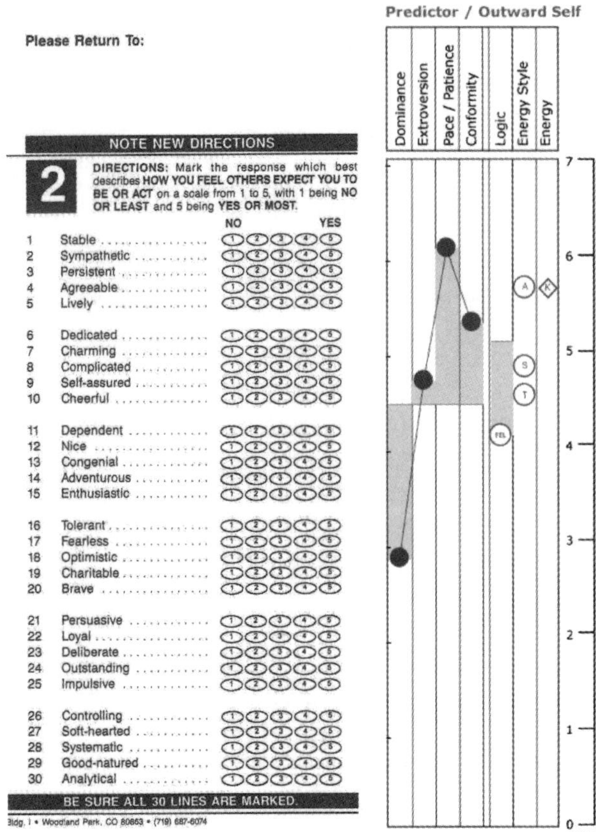

Please Return To:

NOTE NEW DIRECTIONS

2 **DIRECTIONS:** Mark the response which best describes **HOW YOU FEEL OTHERS EXPECT YOU TO BE OR ACT** on a scale from 1 to 5, with 1 being **NO OR LEAST** and 5 being **YES OR MOST**.

		NO				YES
1	Stable	1	2	3	4	5
2	Sympathetic	1	2	3	4	5
3	Persistent	1	2	3	4	5
4	Agreeable	1	2	3	4	5
5	Lively	1	2	3	4	5
6	Dedicated	1	2	3	4	5
7	Charming	1	2	3	4	5
8	Complicated	1	2	3	4	5
9	Self-assured	1	2	3	4	5
10	Cheerful	1	2	3	4	5
11	Dependent	1	2	3	4	5
12	Nice	1	2	3	4	5
13	Congenial	1	2	3	4	5
14	Adventurous	1	2	3	4	5
15	Enthusiastic	1	2	3	4	5
16	Tolerant	1	2	3	4	5
17	Fearless	1	2	3	4	5
18	Optimistic	1	2	3	4	5
19	Charitable	1	2	3	4	5
20	Brave	1	2	3	4	5
21	Persuasive	1	2	3	4	5
22	Loyal	1	2	3	4	5
23	Deliberate	1	2	3	4	5
24	Outstanding	1	2	3	4	5
25	Impulsive	1	2	3	4	5
26	Controlling	1	2	3	4	5
27	Soft-hearted	1	2	3	4	5
28	Systematic	1	2	3	4	5
29	Good-natured	1	2	3	4	5
30	Analytical	1	2	3	4	5

BE SURE ALL 30 LINES ARE MARKED.

Bldg. I • Woodland Park, CO 80863 • (719) 687-6074

Side Two of the ProScan Survey.]

On Side Two, the directions are different from Side One. A person marks the response which best describes HOW YOU FEEL OTHERS EXPECT YOU TO BE OR ACT, on a scale from 1 to 5, with 1 being ***NO OR LEAST*** and 5 being ***YES OR MOST***.

This second set of thirty adjectives measures the Predictor/Outward Self (identified as the "Role-Playing Self"), or how a person comes across to others.

Based on our roles and responsibilities in life as a husband, wife, father, mother, brother, sister, friend, employer, employee, manager, etc., most of us have something pulling or directing us to be more or less of who we are naturally. As we move these traits up or down, those around us believe we are actually this person.

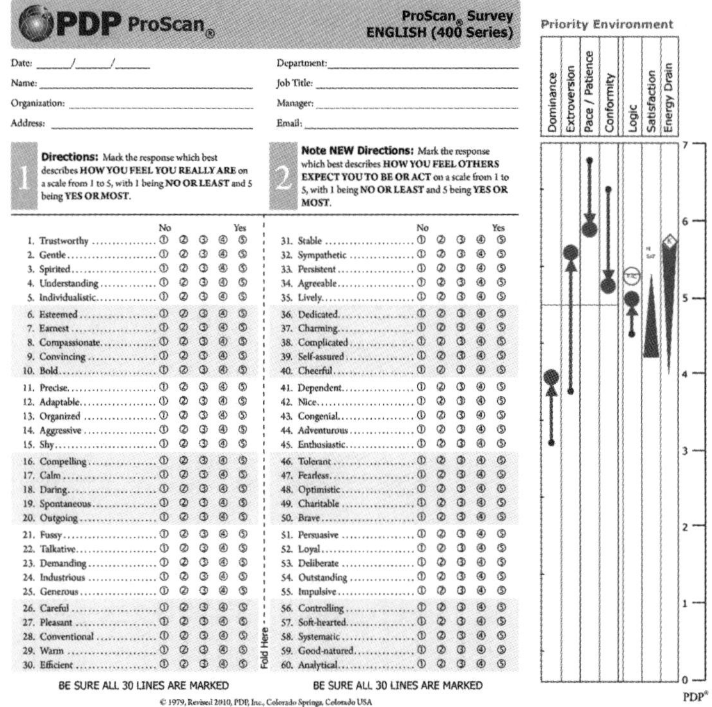

PDP ProScan® — **ProScan® Survey ENGLISH (400 Series)**

Date: ___/___/___ Department: ______
Name: ______ Job Title: ______
Organization: ______ Manager: ______
Address: ______ Email: ______

1 Directions: Mark the response which best describes **HOW YOU FEEL YOU REALLY ARE** on a scale from 1 to 5, with 1 being **NO OR LEAST** and 5 being **YES OR MOST**.

2 Note NEW Directions: Mark the response which best describes **HOW YOU FEEL OTHERS EXPECT YOU TO BE OR ACT** on a scale from 1 to 5, with 1 being **NO OR LEAST** and 5 being **YES OR MOST**.

	No				Yes			No				Yes
1. Trustworthy	①	②	③	④	⑤		31. Stable	①	②	③	④	⑤
2. Gentle	①	②	③	④	⑤		32. Sympathetic	①	②	③	④	⑤
3. Spirited	①	②	③	④	⑤		33. Persistent	①	②	③	④	⑤
4. Understanding	①	②	③	④	⑤		34. Agreeable	①	②	③	④	⑤
5. Individualistic	①	②	③	④	⑤		35. Lively	①	②	③	④	⑤
6. Esteemed	①	②	③	④	⑤		36. Dedicated	①	②	③	④	⑤
7. Earnest	①	②	③	④	⑤		37. Charming	①	②	③	④	⑤
8. Compassionate	①	②	③	④	⑤		38. Complicated	①	②	③	④	⑤
9. Convincing	①	②	③	④	⑤		39. Self-assured	①	②	③	④	⑤
10. Bold	①	②	③	④	⑤		40. Cheerful	①	②	③	④	⑤
11. Precise	①	②	③	④	⑤		41. Dependent	①	②	③	④	⑤
12. Adaptable	①	②	③	④	⑤		42. Nice	①	②	③	④	⑤
13. Organized	①	②	③	④	⑤		43. Congenial	①	②	③	④	⑤
14. Aggressive	①	②	③	④	⑤		44. Adventurous	①	②	③	④	⑤
15. Shy	①	②	③	④	⑤		45. Enthusiastic	①	②	③	④	⑤
16. Compelling	①	②	③	④	⑤		46. Tolerant	①	②	③	④	⑤
17. Calm	①	②	③	④	⑤		47. Fearless	①	②	③	④	⑤
18. Daring	①	②	③	④	⑤		48. Optimistic	①	②	③	④	⑤
19. Spontaneous	①	②	③	④	⑤		49. Charitable	①	②	③	④	⑤
20. Outgoing	①	②	③	④	⑤		50. Brave	①	②	③	④	⑤
21. Fussy	①	②	③	④	⑤		51. Persuasive	①	②	③	④	⑤
22. Talkative	①	②	③	④	⑤		52. Loyal	①	②	③	④	⑤
23. Demanding	①	②	③	④	⑤		53. Deliberate	①	②	③	④	⑤
24. Industrious	①	②	③	④	⑤		54. Outstanding	①	②	③	④	⑤
25. Generous	①	②	③	④	⑤		55. Impulsive	①	②	③	④	⑤
26. Careful	①	②	③	④	⑤		56. Controlling	①	②	③	④	⑤
27. Pleasant	①	②	③	④	⑤		57. Soft-hearted	①	②	③	④	⑤
28. Conventional	①	②	③	④	⑤	Fold Here	58. Systematic	①	②	③	④	⑤
29. Warm	①	②	③	④	⑤		59. Good-natured	①	②	③	④	⑤
30. Efficient	①	②	③	④	⑤		60. Analytical	①	②	③	④	⑤

BE SURE ALL 30 LINES ARE MARKED — BE SURE ALL 30 LINES ARE MARKED

© 1979, Revised 2010, PDP, Inc., Colorado Springs, Colorado USA

The Priority Environment is a combination of both sides of the ProScan survey. Measuring the story of how a person deals with life's stresses and pressures, this in-depth appraisal takes into account both experiences and time. In other words, if you stayed up all night over-stuffing yourself on a pizza, and completed a ProScan in the morning, it would not complicate your results.

Throughout the years, what has amazed people is the fact that it is possible to complete a four-to-six-minute ProScan survey and have it measure such a depth of information—as well as having the ability to so accurately measure the story of how someone is dealing with life's pressures.

I have seen the profile of a person who had previously experienced a heart attack. He was on medication with frequent hospital visits on the treadmill for measuring stress, and his ProScan stress measurement confirmed with the hospital measurements. There was absolutely *no* stress.

Another client retired after a devastating stroke. His ProScan stress measurement indicated extreme stress and energy burnout, but he failed to recognize his situations and kept on working without making any adjustments.

In fact, the ProScan comprehensive report has proven to be priceless to those who seek the wisdom of understanding just about any situation where people are involved.

Like an X-Ray or MRI Experience

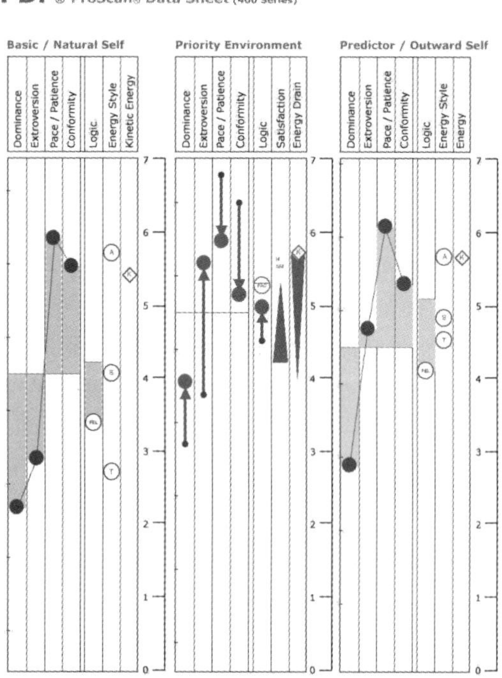

One of the most impressive reports from the PDPWorks system is the one-page "Data Sheet." On the Data Sheet, a graph provides the visual description of PDP's measurements of a person's three environments: the Basic/Natural Self, Priority Environment, and Predictor/Outward Self. For the trained administrator, the Data Sheet provides behavioral information comparable to medical professionals having an X-Ray or an MRI of a patient. The resulting information simply provides the knowledge and authority of knowing a person quickly—and with precision.

The founder of PDP, Bruce M. Hubby, often described the Data Sheet experience with one of his favorite expressions—"a picture is worth a thousand words"—saying that a glimpse of a Data Sheet is comparable to a "behavioral photograph."

Understanding How the Traits Perform

To have an understanding of a person's Cornerstone Traits (or Basic Performance Traits) is the beginning of understanding, but the real value comes from application. The most dangerous position an administrator can take is to revert to "pigeon holing" or placing another person into a box based on a simple impression of who they are and how they interact with others. Based on our natural behaviors, we have an instinct to place others into a pattern of definition of what is best for them, how to communicate with them, and what our own expectations are.

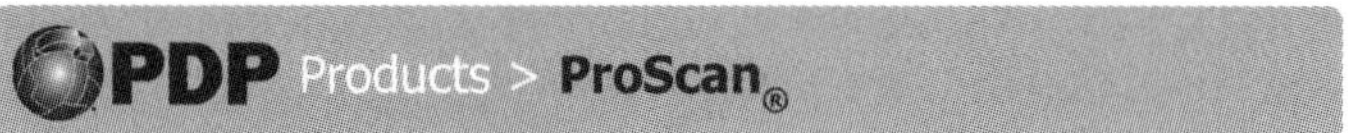

Basic Performance Traits

Each trait has its own value, specific strengths, and unique place in the world.

DOMINANCE		EXTROVERSION	
Description Competitive Controlling and authoritative To the point Risk taker and decisive		Description Outgoing, empathetic Persuasive Enthusiastic, motivating Organization builders	
Wants Direct answers Challenge Authority, power Bottom line results	Doesn't Want External controls Trivial interferences	Wants Recognition Status Favorable working environment Opportunities Team involvement	Doesn't Want To be unappreciated Rejection Isolation
Speaking Direct Authoritative Takes charge Confrontational Tells it like it is	Listening Needs concise, direct messages Likes innovative, problem-solving ideas Dislikes repeated details	Speaking Persuasive Positive Articulate Constantly aware of others	Listening Responds to approval Wants recognition Wants discussion about ideas, issues, growth No insults
PACE		**CONFORMITY**	
Description Persistent Dependable Cooperative Harmonious Thorough		Description Procedural Precise Loyal Systematic	
Wants Stability Predictability Benefits Consensus	Doesn't Want Unjustified pressure Sudden change Conflict Insincerity	Wants Structure Accuracy Security Proven systems	Doesn't Want Unjustified criticism High risk actions
Speaking Careful Non-confrontational Patient Tolerant Attitude of wait and see	Listening Takes time to hear details Wants time to think it through Needs clear goals and expectations	Speaking Conscientious Cautious Concerned Detailed	Listening Wants clearly defined directions Wants respect and sincere praise Prefers written guidelines and frequent updates

Simplicity is a Beautiful Thing

From conception to execution, the ProScan survey process delivers unprecedented clarity with robust possibilities that help us to understand human behavior. Many people desire to improve their lives not knowing that it is related to their behavior. Maybe we wish we could control our dietary behaviors to lose weight, improve our golf score to match our skill level, or control our spending and saving habits.

Usually, decisions originate in our minds and the results are exhibited in our behaviors. If we can make concerted efforts because of a strong desire to want something badly enough, our behaviors can be adjusted into positive change. However, this is almost fruitless without first knowing which behaviors we need to modify—and how far they need to move for positive change.

Age and Behavioral Development

The formation of behavior begins with the child in the womb and develops with time, influences and experiences. Here are the age categories to provide a scale.

> "Age 0 to 18 - Conditioning Period. Extremely vulnerable to the influence of others.
>
> Age 19 to 28 - Maturation Period. During these ages there is a solidifying of the traits, however, this period is flexible to change.
>
> Age 29 to 38 - Solidification Period. During these years, a behavior is quite fixed, changed only by an important emotional event.
>
> Age 39 to 42 - Re-evaluation Period.

Age 43 to 62 - Fixed Period. During these years behavioral traits become firmly established.

Age 63 and older - Permanent or "Cast in Bronze" Period."[13]

Note: A significant emotional event can happen to anyone of any age which may result in a change of behavior.

On a particular business trip, I was invited to the home of a client for dinner and to meet his family. After our meal, the host asked if we could ProScan his wife and three children. The youngest was three months shy of her sixth birthday. Although her early age is unusual, I felt she was advanced for her age. A more common early age for experiencing the survey depends on the reading and comprehension skills of the child. After moving from the dining room table to the living room floor, she proceeded to look up the meaning of each of the sixty words on the ProScan survey from their family dictionary.

Curiously, I entered her ProScan scores into the computer and described the child's behavior to her parents. The mother cried from the confirmation of accuracy while the father just smiled. Even at this very young age the assessment was precise as we had an unforgettable conversation discussing how she felt helping her mother around the house as a mother's helper. Her mother had an unusual disease where she felt tired all the time. As she matures through her education and experiences, her behavior will be molded and these behaviors measured by her ProScan will be a snapshot like a photo of her childhood. As a parent, imagine the value of learning the confirmation of your child's behavior at any age.

13 PDP Research Reference Manual, Copyright 1984, rev. 2011, Page 7.3

Chapter Nugget

The most valuable insight we each can possess is an open mind to discover life's possibilities. Applying smart technology is easier—and less expensive—than living in doubt, simply because something doesn't seem feasible. A lack of knowledge becomes obvious when it is least expected.

"Man's mind stretched to a new idea never goes back to its original dimensions."
-- Oliver Wendell Holmes

CHAPTER 12

THE INVENTOR

Bruce M. Hubby, 1993, Cripple Creek, Colorado, photo taken by Kathleen Crosby.]

In the fall of 1991, I met Dr. Bonnie Bass, who introduced me to her brother, Bruce M. Hubby, the Founder and President of PDP. At the time, I did not realize that this incredible ProScan behavioral technology was the "Holy Grail" that would eventually become my vocation. For most of my life, I had been searching for the answers to "the why" I do what I do. Now, I have found them, and want to share them with anyone who has ever had similar desires, concerns, or aspirations. Today, almost twenty-five years after our first meeting, Bruce's influence as a friend and mentor has deeply affected my life, neatly fitting into a plan of destiny to fulfill my passion.

Rather than describing the intertwining complexity of the ProScan tool, its validity, and the history behind its impressiveness, I have chosen to introduce all of this through the voice of the inventor, Bruce M. Hubby.[14]

Research Overview by Bruce M. Hubby (1984)

Two major domains of research exist. One is primarily academic, while one occupies the commercial world. PDP's primary purpose is to market a superior instrument that was developed using the skills of academics combined with case studies from the business world. All research was accomplished through private funding. For this reason, PDP trade secrets are jealously guarded and only limited publishing, if any, is considered.

This philosophy has created the difficult challenge of sharing enough research to satisfy those that are research-oriented while still protecting proprietary information that cost hundreds of thousands of dollars to develop. Bibliographies from "Monographs 1–10" are con-

14 *A Living Legacy: The Man, the Research, the System*, 2nd ed (Colorado Springs, CO: PDP, Inc., 2013), ch 3. Used with permission.

clusive phase studies. PDP's research includes studies from the 1930s through the 1970s, as well as referencing other well-known personality concepts including Hippocrates's traits of behavior (Melancholy, Sanguine, Choleric, Phlegmatic, 400 BC), King Solomon's "as a man thinketh," and Pavlov's habituated reaction to stimuli. Research material on these subjects is readily available.

The PDP Integrated Management System is a computer-dependent factor analysis concept that originally targeted descriptors of purest factor loading (or single complexity). PDP first proved its accuracy through the academic criteria of validation (construct, content, concurrent, and predictive), reliability (split-half and test-retest), structural invariance, factor inter-correlations, and intrinsic/extrinsic validity. Once reliability was established, in 1978 PDP launched a major practical field-norming program that now totals over 6 million. Certainly, the true test was customer satisfaction—broad positive responses and continued usage of the system—which have been most gratifying to PDP as the developer.

In contrast to all—or nearly all—similar personality systems, PDP originated as a statistically validated (quantitative) instrument as opposed to originating as a theory-origin (cognitive) system. Factor analysis, which is advanced statistics in any university curriculum, is very simply defined as a matrix system for independently determining the isolated purity of, in this case, an adjective or descriptor. Once factor analysis was completed, the next step was to find groupings with components of like purity (primary factor loading) and to consult with experts to identify the behavioral factor or trait. Starting with descriptors (185 adjectives in "Monographs 1–4," 1977–78) associated with behavioral studies drawn from those of Thurstone (1934), Cattell (1950), Guilford (1954), Fiske (1949), Daniels (1973), Horst (1978), and PDP (1978), sixty descriptors were identified, and all exhibited high factor loadings for each of the primary factors in the instrument.

After the statistical work had been completed, intense fieldwork followed to develop case studies best to describe the behavior of people with like responses to trait clusters. The type and degree of behavior was determined by two dimensions: (1) the comparable amount of trait intensity from a base of zero, and (2) the amplitude variance from the individual's own norm (*Fundamental Research Statistics for the Behavioral Sciences*, J. T. Roscoe). A fixed-norm system was used only in the primary graphing and later as a point of interest. Most instruments do not get beyond the fixed-norming method, thus missing the values of sensitivity, satisfaction, stress analysis, stress management, logic, and other lesser factors.

Chapter Nugget

From the beginning of time, scholars have dedicated their lives to developing knowledgeable theories, and from these minds of genius have come powerful contributions.

> "Instead of the labels of tests, assessments or evaluations, the ProScan Survey offers a sense of respectful and dynamic opportunity for people to identify personal characteristics."
>
> -- Dr. Bonnie D. Bass

FINAL THOUGHTS

Now that you have read some of my stories, as told in Chapters 1-4, I invite you to follow me by perhaps writing your own memoirs or even journaling some of your childhood recollections.

As you prepare, realize that learning about *The Why You Do* includes contemplating your early story, no matter how joyful or painful. Just take a deep breath and work through it. Trace the earliest memories from your youth to your adulthood while traveling the "yellow brick road" with interesting characters, and describe how your life was affected by your experiences. Even if there were influences or situations that has affected your personal identity by your choices, you are not flawed by God's perfect design. Once you understand your intrinsic behavior through the ProScan assessment, it will provide the knowledge and clarity to help you with your "Life Blueprint" as you grow and expand your ambitions. The ability to thoroughly understand your own behavior is the beginning of learning how to succeed, because the internal mechanisms we use to process information are behaviorally based.

If you're uncomfortable—or dissatisfied—with your personal identity, hopefully, the acronym "DACI" will encourage you. Here is what it stands for:

- **D**iscover and learn about who you are. Don't be fearful; be proactive.
- **A**ccept who you are, in spite of what you may have heard growing up. Forgive, forget, and expand your horizons.
- **C**elebrate your behavioral design. Match your behavior with your passion and make a significant difference.
- **I**nside is what counts. Don't judge yourself by your appearance or compare yourself to others. It's up to you to make a difference, but do it with compassion and courage.

Life embraces us all as a comprised collection of roles and responsibilities. Some are life-altering with relationships, families, businesses, careers and volunteer positions. There have been rewarding life lessons both with victories and with loss.

By knowing yourself with your ProScan assessment this fulfills the question of personal identification, then coincided with life experiences provides your story. This equation of understanding behavior and history has empowered my life, and now my hope is that it will also provide you with the ease and application of how to live your lives successfully.

> "Never forget that you are one of a kind. Never forget that if there weren't any need for you in all your uniqueness to be on this earth, you wouldn't be here in the first place. And never forget, no matter how overwhelming life's challenges and problems seem to be, that one person can make a difference in the world. In fact, it is always because of one person that all the changes that matter in the world come about. So be that one person."
>
> -- R. Buckminster Fuller

ACKNOWLEDGMENTS

This book was inspired by gratitude to my family and friends, and urgently motivated by the quick passage of time, in an effort to preserve these experiences, stories, and nuggets before they became nothing more than unprinted memories.

I lovingly dedicate this collection of words to my bride and Polynesian Princess, Kathleen, who, for thirty years, has unselfishly given me her unconditional love to ensure that our life together would showcase a Godly marriage. I am eternally grateful.

To my father, the late J. E. Crosby, the finest man I ever met—an extraordinary person with a gentle disposition and lovely heart. Thank you for your exemplary work ethic and for being the best "Dad" you knew how to be.

To my mother, Mary Frances Dunn, whose thoughtfulness and concern for everyone around us never kept her from taking care of our family and teaching me well. I am deeply indebted to you for your encouragement throughout my painful experiences (even those you did not know of) and for insisting that I reach my God-given potential. You and Dad had vastly different qualities, but you both were incredible role models—and I am proud to be your son.

My sincere appreciation goes to the late Bruce M. Hubby, founder of Professional DynaMetric Programs (PDP). If it were not for your vision to create the finest behavioral measurement tools known to our profession, and your steadfast accomplishments, I question where my career path would have gone. Thank you for your friendship, mentoring skills, and supreme confidence, as well as the priceless times we have shared.

Lastly, I wish to thank Victor Bellarosa for his genuine kindness during my darkest days—when he noticed a neighbor struggling and witnessed the simplicity of God's love. With his calm and focused manner of telling his story, he laid the foundation for changing the outcome of mine.

August 30, 1994

To Whom It May Concern:

It gives me great pleasure as President to record the official opinion of PDP, Inc. as "par excellence" in the representing of PDP by Donald James Associates as a Franchisee. In nearly 16 years of franchising, we have not seen a team so eager, honest, organized or image conscious. Mr. Crosby's big picture, professional image, staff and quality materials complement all the materials of PDP and are certain to be major factors for developing a mutually beneficial and long lasting relationship.

The strength of the DJA group seems to be in their marketing and packaging, resulting in a unique service to a large array of organizational needs both locally and internationally.

Sincerely,

Bruce M. Hubby
President

BMH:jcp

PDP Inc., Corporate Offices • 400 West Highway 24 • Suite 201 • Box 5289 • Woodland Park, Colorado 80866
Telephone (719) 687-6074 • FAX (719) 687-8587

PDP Global
13710 Struthers Road, Suite 215
Colorado Springs, Colorado USA 80921
Tel. 719.785.7300 • Fax 719.687.8587
WEB www.PDPglobal.com • APP www.PDPworks.com

July 28, 2014

Don Crosby
Global Behavior
P.O. Box 49496
Charlotte, NC 28277

Dear Don:

"It is my distinct pleasure to endorse **"The Why You Do"** – a 360-degree perspective candidly written by my friend, Don Crosby – that revolves within the community of behavioral science, without becoming a hard-to-read textbook. Receiving his manuscript was truly a thrill as we have had countless hours of conversation about his dream of sharing these stories and real-life experiences with others. His dream has come true!

As I reflect upon our first meeting in the early 1990s in Honolulu, Hawaii, little did I know that Don and I would develop such a solid personal and business relationship. Since the very beginning, Don was an eager-to-learn student who has grown into a valuable teacher and mentor. The number of nationwide organizations he has transformed and the personal lives he has positively influenced by using the PDP ProScan® Survey are remarkable. Whatever the situation, Don is able to apply the appropriate guidance, consultation, and expertise. He steps in and encourages client organizations to tap into the full potential of their people by licensing the PDP System in-house.

Don is a beacon of PDP light in the world and helps organizations and individuals attain their goals. He continues to impress me with his knowledge and wisdom in applying PDP with stellar results – from saving companies from closure to increasing profits greatly, or saving failing marriages to reigniting love in healthy relationships, and so much more.

"The Why You Do" resonates with the passion and vision that my father, Bruce M. Hubby, founder of PDP, had for opening the eyes of the world to the brilliance of *who* someone is and *why* they do what they do. Enjoy!

Sincerely,

Brent W. Hubby
President
PDP Global

ABOUT THE AUTHOR

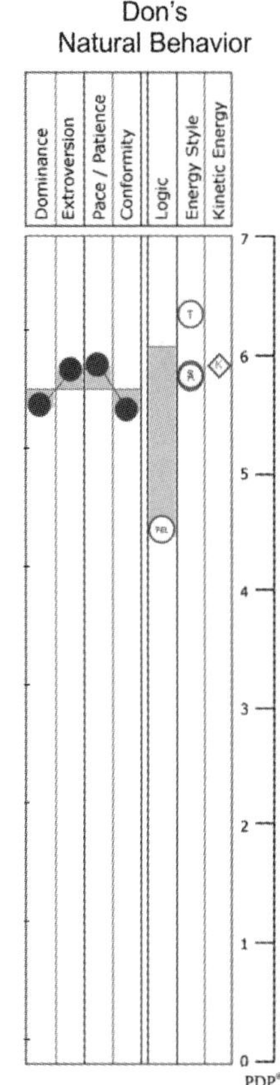

Don Crosby is Founder/CEO of Global Behavior Companies and is known as the "Behavioral Locksmith." During his more than twenty-four years of consulting and training experience, Don has successfully assessed thousands of people while working with small, medium, and Fortune 500 companies.

Don has established himself as an accomplished speaker and a popular choice for organizations holding workshops, seminars, and retreats, while consulting and training on the concepts of human behavior and "The Why you do." Don's passion for people can be heard first- hand on his podcast and syndicated radio talk show, *Sound Behavior*. Motivated with a strong dedication to improving the caliber of one's understanding of their natural dynamics and impacting relationships, Don has a profound, insightful ability to help organizations get the best out of their most important asset: *their people.*

Don and his bride Kathleen are celebrating thirty years of marriage. They reside in Charlotte, NC, with Jerry, their cocker spaniel, and travel extensively helping people unlock their behavioral misunderstandings for impacting relationships.

LEARN ABOUT "THE WHY YOU DO"

Benefit by the opportunity to receive your personal ProScan assessment for a special offer at www.MyProScan.com.

You can order the book about Bruce M. Hubby, *A Living Legacy: The Man, the Research, the System*, at www.doncrosby.net.

Services Available

Learn how Don's services, including the following, can become a priceless component for your success strategy.

- Business Systems, Consultation and Certification Training
- Pubic Speaking Engagements
- Mentor Training Certification
- Representative Business Opportunities
- Beyond Our Love Marriage Events

Don Crosby, Founder/CEO
Global Behavior Companies, LLC
P.O. Box 49496, Charlotte, NC 28277
www.GlobalBehavior.com - www.DonCrosby.net
service@globalbehavior.com
704.918.1013